CULTURE SMART!
JAPAN

Paul Norbury

·K·U·P·E·R·A·R·D·

This book is available for special discounts for bulk purchases for sales promotions or premiums. Special editions, including personalized covers, excerpts of existing books, and corporate imprints, can be created in large quantities for special needs.

For more information contact Kuperard publishers at the address below.

ISBN 978 1 85733 860 7
This book is also available as an e-book: eISBN 978 1 85733 861 4
British Library Cataloguing in Publication Data
A CIP catalogue entry for this book is available from the British Library

First published in Great Britain
by Kuperard, an imprint of Bravo Ltd
59 Hutton Grove, London N12 8DS
Tel: +44 (0) 20 8446 2440   Fax: +44 (0) 20 8446 2441
www.culturesmart.co.uk
Inquiries: sales@kuperard.co.uk

Series Editor Geoffrey Chesler
Design Bobby Birchall

Printed in Malaysia

About the Author

PAUL NORBURY has been closely associated with Japan and Asian Studies as publisher, editor, and author since the early 1970s, principally through his various imprints: Paul Norbury Publications, Japan Library, Global Oriental, and most recently Renaissance Books. In 2003 he received the Japan Society Award, in 2011 the Order of the Rising Sun (Japanese government), and in 2013 the Order of Civic Virtue (government of the Republic of Sakha, Yakutia, Russian Commonwealth). He is also the author of *Culture Smart! Britain.*

**The Culture Smart! series is continuing to expand.
For further information and latest titles visit
www.culturesmart.co.uk**

The publishers would like to thank **CultureSmart!**Consulting for its help in researching and developing the concept for this series.

CultureSmart!Consulting creates tailor-made seminars and consultancy programs to meet a wide range of corporate, public-sector, and individual needs. Whether delivering courses on multicultural team building in the USA, preparing Chinese engineers for a posting in Europe, training call-center staff in India, or raising the awareness of police forces to the needs of diverse ethnic communities, it provides essential, practical, and powerful skills worldwide to an increasingly international workforce.

For details, visit www.culturesmartconsulting.com

CultureSmart!Consulting and **CultureSmart!** guides have both contributed to and featured regularly in the weekly travel program "Fast Track" on BBC World TV.

contents

contents

Map of Japan

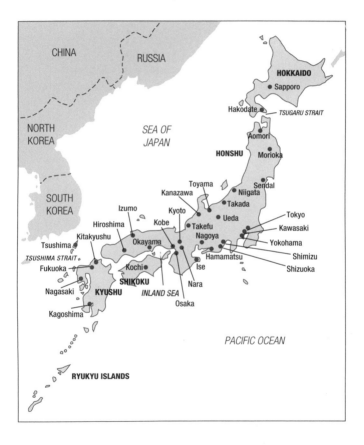

introduction

Japan is often thought of as a "far away" country where they do things differently, and this is indeed true. The Japanese have, for example, a unique language not shared by any other group of people, and a unique religion—Shinto; but for a combination of reasons, including the ease of international travel, the impact of global trading, and the Internet, Japan is becoming increasingly "Western" in its norms, expectations, and way of life, and its young people welcome that. Japan today participates more widely in the international arenas of sport, music, food, fashion, design, robotics, R&D collaboration, overseas aid, and "soft power" diplomacy than ever before. In 2020 it will host the XXXII Olympiad.

However, despite this pursuit of so-called modern living, the core values of traditional Japan—a sense of duty rather than of rights, the pursuit of harmony as an instinctive need at all levels of society, and respect for each other throughout life, and not least in old age—endure. The visitor should be aware that notions of "uniqueness" also endure in the Japanese psyche. Japan is one of the most pleasant and safest countries to live in; it has one of the best medical infrastructures, and enjoys the longest life expectancy in the world

Japan functions mainly as a consensus-based society, but Japanese genius and eccentricity point to an unexpected strand of individualism. Perhaps most importantly, what appears to be the innate aesthetic sensibility of the Japanese is evident everywhere—in their literature, arts and crafts, gardens and buildings, design, and technology. Yet, there is a striking paradox here that the visitor needs to prepare for, viz., the sprawling ugliness of metropolitan Japan that manages to challenge all the senses!

Beyond the current preoccupations of faltering economic growth, and concerns relating to security and climate change, shared with much of the industrialized world, Japan today finds itself engaged with other issues revolving around the so-called "modernizing" government of Prime Minister Abe Shinzō, looking to "restore" Japan's national pride, its economy, and its role in the world—all in the context of a declining and rapidly aging population. Abe's sweeping victory in the Upper House in July 2016, virtually ensures an attempt to change Japan's peace constitution, including the article renouncing war, which will be put to a referendum.

Nevertheless, regardless of Mr Abe's political agenda, Japan's democratic foundations are solid. Furthermore, its economy is the third-largest in the world and it remains one of the most attractive and secure destinations for investment. It continues to excel at innovation in technology and the "new" sciences, and is among the world's largest funders in research as a percentage of GDP. It may be unrealistic to suggest that the Japanese economy is going to return to its former glory in the near future; but given its historical resilience, both in terms of managing one of the world's most challenging natural environments and its capacity to embrace change, Japan will surely continue to be a major player on the world stage.

The resilience, coherence, and consensus-based structure of Japanese society—once seen by some as a country "where nothing changes"—are increasingly regarded as virtues in a world of accelerating change and instability. This new, updated edition of *Culture Smart! Japan*, will guide you through Japan's shifting social and cultural maze. It provides information and insights into people's attitudes and behavior and practical advice to help you discover the brilliance and charm of this complex, rich, and dynamic society.

Key Facts

Official Name	*Nippon*	Japan
Capital City	Tokyo	Population, (23 wards) 9.24 million (2015)
Main Cities	Osaka, Nagoya, Kobe, Yokohama, Fukuoka, Sapporo	
Area	143,660 square miles (372,079 sq.km.)	Japan uses the metric system.
Climate	Moist temperate	
Currency	Yen	Paper: Yen10,000, 5000, and 1000 Coins: Yen 500, 100, 50, 10, 5, and 1
Population	126 million	
Ethnic Makeup	Approx. 98.5% Japanese; Approx. 1.5 % others	Other principal nationalities: Korean, Chinese, Brazilian
Family Makeup	Average family size is 2.62 people. Birthrate: 1.43	In opinion polls, over 80% of Japanese perceive themselves as middle class.
Language	*Nihongo* (Japanese)	Principal other languages taught in schools: English, French, Spanish, and German
Religion	No state religion. Most Japanese are both Shinto and Buddhist.	1.5% are Christians. Increasing interest in new religious movements

Government	Japan is a constitutional monarchy. It has universal adult suffrage (from age 20), a written Constitution, and is a parliamentary democracy with an upper and a lower chamber (Representatives in lower house with 511 seats, and Councillors in upper house with 252 seats, both elected). The parliament is known as the National Diet. According to the 1946 Constitution, the Emperor is "the symbol of the state and unity of the people." Japan has 47 prefectures. Prefectural governors, as well as city, town, and village mayors are all elected.	
Media	NHK (Japan Broadcasting System) is Japan's public broadcasting corporation.	There are more than 100 daily newspapers, led by *Yomiuri, Asahi, Mainichi, Nihon Keizai*, and *Sankei*.
Media: English Language	English-language newspapers (print and online) include: *The Japan Times, Mainichi, Japan Today, The Japan News, International New York Times*	
Electricity	100 & 200 volts (50 cycles in eastern Japan, incl. Tokyo; 60 cycles in the west, incl. Nagoya, Kyoto, and Osaka).	Plugs are flat 2-pin. Adaptors required
Video TV	NTSC 525-line system	Compatible with US but not UK
Internet Domain	.jp	
Telephone	Japan's country code is 81.	The dial-out code for international calls depends on the provider: 001 for KDD, 0041 for ITJ, or 0061 for IDC.

chapter one

LAND & PEOPLE

LOCATION

The Japanese archipelago, situated in the North Pacific to the east of Korea, consists of four main islands—Hokkaido, Honshu (the largest, with 60 percent of the landmass), Shikoku (the smallest), and Kyushu—which together make up 98 percent of the country's territory. The remainder is made up of a number of small islands, including the Ryukus (of which Okinawa is one), which lie strung out in the Pacific between Kagoshima in southern Kyushu and Taiwan; in addition, there are some 3,000 tiny islets that surround the coastline and extend southward.

Overall, Japan is slightly smaller than France or Spain, but slightly larger than Italy or the British Isles, and accounts for 0.3 percent of the world's landmass. The "arc" of its primary archipelago extends from 30°N in southern Kyushu to 45°N in northern Hokkaido, a latitudinal range comparable to the Atlantic seaboard of the USA from Maine to Florida, or in Europe, from Venice to Cairo; if we include the string of southern islands (such as Okinawa), which reach as far south as latitude 20, the distance covered is 2,362 miles (3,800 kilometers).

The Tsushima Strait (known as the Kaikyo Strait in Korea), which separates Japan from Korea, is 112 miles (180 kilometers) wide, while some

500 miles (800 kilometers) of open sea lie between southwestern Japan and the nearest point on the coast of China.

THE LAND

Running through the center of Japan—endowing it with a rare scenic beauty—are six chains of steep, serrated mountains that are studded with volcanoes resulting from her geological location within the Pacific "ring of fire." There are over 100 volcanoes, some seventy-seven of which are designated as "active" (although few really are), especially Bandai and Asama in central Honshu, Aso, Unzen, and Sakurajima, which is currently in an active phase, in Kyushu. The highest is Fuji (known as *Fuji-san*), standing at 12,388 feet (3,776 meters), which last erupted in 1707 but is still on the "active" list. In central Japan, dense mixed forests of oak, beech, and maple blanket the slopes up to an altitude of 5,900 feet (1,800 meters).

Land shortage, particularly during the period of spectacular economic growth in the second half of the twentieth century, concentrated minds on the potential for land reclamation. This hugely expensive and painstaking process took place in many parts of Japan (and continues to do so), adding valuable new building land (approximately 0.5 percent) to Japan's main landmass of 143,660 square miles (372,070 square kilometers); it included vast areas around the modern industrial cities of Tokyo (especially Tokyo Bay) and Osaka. Most remarkable was the creation of Port Island and Rokko Island, and other adjacent islands, off the port of Kobe, as well as the new Kansai International Airport (which is known to be sinking at the rate of 2.5 in (7 cm) per year) involving the removal of millions of tons of earth and rocks from the tops of neighboring mountains—a solution that underlines the pragmatic Japanese approach to life and its challenges. On the other hand, all of Japan's coastal areas are at risk (the Inland Sea less so) from storm damage and *tsunami*—the giant waves generated by earthquake activity which the people of northeastern Japan (Tohoku region) learnt to their terrible cost in the great earthquake of 2011 (see page 17).

CLIMATE AND SEASONS

Many people have found it ironic that the refined aesthetics, the exquisite art forms and cultural elegance of Japan (consider, for example, the manicured beauty of her formal gardens!) should have been created in a group of islands that straddle one of the world's most dangerous tectonic regions—four tectonic plates, the North American, the Pacific, the Eurasian, and the Philippine, meet under the Japanese archipelago—and in one of its most hazardous climatic zones. Japan's climate is the outcome of two competing weather systems, one from the Pacific and one from Continental Asia, involving, at times, ferocious annual weather changes from deep snow and low temperatures to devastating typhoons and unbearable levels of humidity. These physical facts heighten interest in what can generally be called the "Japanese achievement" throughout history.

The Japanese themselves regard such notions of "achievement," however, as transient and very fragile, likening them, as with life itself, to the brief flowering of the cherry blossom (*sakura*) in spring. They celebrate this natural phenomenon with outdoor events, public and private "viewings," and the writing of poetry. As the countryside warms up, the blossoming fans out in an extraordinary six-week flourish, initially from southern Kyushu in early March, then on through Shikoku and Honshu to northern Hokkaido, along a 1,100-mile (1,800-kilometer) journey.

Seasonal changes, therefore, are well defined and vary considerably from east to west and from mountain to plain. In Tokyo, which sits on the Kanto Plain, the biggest of the coastal plains, the average temperature is 77 °F (25 °C) in summer with high humidity and 38 °F (4 °C) in winter. The sunniest months are December and January; the wettest June and September. Spring (March to May) and fall (mid-September to end-November) are considered to be the best months because the days are generally clear and sunny with sharp blue skies—the fall, like New England, having the added attraction of the leaves, especially the maple, turning to red and gold. Like the cherry blossom viewing, the fall colors are also celebrated with outings and excursions.

Seasons apart, it is worth remembering that Japan is often "wet" and, like the UK, is an "umbrella" society! Indeed, umbrellas are to be found everywhere in case of need—in hotels, offices, restaurants, and temples.

EARTHQUAKES

Earthquakes are frequent and widespread, and although most are mild and hardly noticeable, the threat of catastrophe is ever present—as was demonstrated in recent times by the Kobe earthquake of January 1995, the devastating earthquake and tsunami off the east coast near the city of Sendai, Tohoku Prefecture, in March 2011, and the Kumamoto earthquakes of April 2016.

Whenever a serious tremor occurs, city gas supplies are automatically cut off; all commercially available oil heaters have extinguishing mechanisms. Each district organizes earthquake drills on a regular basis, and all households are supposed to keep an emergency survival kit, available from department stores. All hotels are also required to follow such drills and are rigorously scrutinized for safety in both design and exit procedure. Following the Tohoku catastrophe, all systems were up for review.

RICE AND FISH

Heavy rains and hot summers allow rice, Japan's staple food, to be grown on most of the lowlands, including, surprisingly, the northern island of

THE EARTHQUAKE OF 2011

Japan's worst-ever recorded earthquake (9.0 on the Richter Scale) took place on March 11, 2011 at 2:46 p.m. local time. Its epicenter was 81 miles (130.4 kilometers) off the east coast, near the city of Sendai. The tsunami that followed reached unimagined heights —especially at Mayuko City where it reached a height of 128 feet (39 meters) —causing catastrophic damage to towns and villages along 350 miles (563 kilometers) of the northeast coast, some completely wiped out, with the confirmed loss of some 15,900 lives with 2,500 still missing. The impact of this devastation was exacerbated by sub-zero temperatures, making access for the recovery teams even harder, as well as by the longer-term worry of radiation leaks from the nuclear power station complex at Fukushima that was also inundated. (Fortunately, radiation levels turned out to be much lower than first feared.)

The process of economic and social recovery is slow and is likely to take more than a generation, with some communities unlikely to return. What the world witnessed was how the Japanese people responded to the terrible trauma with such remarkable courage, dignity, and acceptance.

Most recently, in April 2016 were the two Kumamoto earthquakes in the southern island of Kyushu in in which over 40 people died and over 3,000 were injured. As far as Tokyo is concerned, which has a population of over 9 million, (in its 23 wards) seismologists continue to anticipate the next event on the basis of a notional seventy-year cycle. Tokyo last suffered a major earthquake on September 1, 1923.

Hokkaido (famous also for its potato-growing, and for its winter ice-carving festival), is now one of the main rice-producing areas. As over 70 percent of Japan's landmass is mountain forest, leaving less than a quarter of the land flat enough for human settlement and agriculture, the Japanese have over the centuries perfected the art of paddy-field terracing. In southern Japan these rise in spectacular flights up the mountainsides, presenting from the air a remarkable, intricate lace pattern.

Rice as a staple food has many benefits, not least because it can be grown in the same field year after year. It is also low in cholesterol. In addition, for centuries, right up to the Meiji Restoration of 1868, it was used as a currency, going back to the eighth century when Japan was divided up into sixty-eight administrative districts or provinces by Prince Shotoku. The reputations and well-being of these districts depended on the amount of rice they could produce, and they were taxed accordingly (in rice of course). Not surprisingly, the Japanese government continues to protect Japan's rice-growers, paying up to ten times the world price, in order to maintain the status quo—and, supposedly, the Japanese way of life. (The main crop grown is a short grain white rice—*rice Japonica*—which is sticky when cooked and easily eaten with chopsticks.)

The other Japanese staple is fish, providing up to 50 percent of their protein intake, although meat consumption, along with carbohydrates, has been growing steadily in recent years. The Japanese also love squid, shrimps, king crabs, and many other kinds of seafood caught locally by small fishing boats throughout the islands. This is in addition to the deep-sea fishing for tuna and, more controversially, whale, although it is clear from history that whale meat as such was eaten only by isolated communities; mostly, it was left as carrion. Much was done, however, with whalebone, especially its use in a wide variety of implements, including female coiffure. The wide consumption of whale meat is a relatively recent development resulting from the advances in fishing technology and fleet management. The Japanese government allows whaling for "scientific purposes," which is legal according to the 1986 International Whaling Commision moritorium on commercial whaling, but it remains a contentious issue.

The greatest fish delicacies are to be found in the form of *sashimi*, slices of raw fish spiced with soy sauce, *wasabi* (like horseraddish) and radish (*daikon*), and *sushi* (small pieces of raw fish centered on a small rice "roll" usually wrapped in dried seaweed), now widely appreciated in the West (see Chapter 7).

Supporting traditional fishing is a huge aquaculture industry, farming many types of fish, together with oysters, mussels, and shrimps, as well as growing edible seaweeds in sheltered waters or in tanks and ponds.

"CONNECTING" JAPAN

The requirements of modern life and political expediency have created a demand for increasingly easy access to Japan's four main islands. This has resulted in some of the world's most remarkable engineering feats, especially the building of the Seikan Tunnel, opened after twenty years in 1988, connecting Honshu to Hokkaido. It is 33.5 miles (54 kilometers) long from end to end. Connecting Honshu to Shikoku is a series of three groups of suspension bridges, including the world's longest, the Akashi bridge, which has six lanes and measures 4,277 yards (3,911 meters).

THE JAPANESE PEOPLE: A BRIEF HISTORY
Origins

Although scholars debate endlessly about where the Japanese came from, there is broad agreement that they are a subgroup of the Mongoloid peoples who inhabit large parts of Asia and the New World. This is evident from a skin color that is pale to light brown, straight black hair, brown eyes, and a relative lack of body hair, as well as a high frequency of such features as epicanthic eyes (the absence of a fold on the upper eyelid). Nevertheless, the Japanese differ as much as any other ethnic group from individual to individual in both facial characteristics and physique.

It is also accepted that, although culturally Japan may be described as "a daughter of China," the Japanese are not Chinese. The Japanese reached Japan by a variety of routes, including Korea, and at some point around the seventh to eighth century the "mixing" process was complete, resulting in the Japanese people we know today. (This "mix" includes descendants of the Yamato and even the Yayoi people, described below. Unfortunately, there is very little archaeological evidence to substantiate any particular thesis. New finds are reported regularly—some subsequently exposed as frauds— and scholars continue to hope that they will be allowed full access to the early burial mounds, such as that of the legendary Emperor Nintoku of the early fifth century, near Osaka, which is the largest keyhole-shaped tomb in Japan.). But the Imperial Household Agency which has responsibility for the tombs is unlikely to agree to any excavation or examination of the bodies for the forseeable future.

However, a quite separate and distinct minority race known as the Ainu (a Caucasian group, probably from mainland Siberia) settled in northern Japan over twelve hundred years ago; today they live principally in Hokkaido, where their traditional language and culture is protected.

Recently, remarkable archaeological finds have shown that southern Japan, especially northern Kyushu and the Inland Sea, were settled by Stone Age groups who were skilled hunters and gatherers many thousands of years BCE. This is known as the Jomon (rope pattern) period, distinguished by pottery vessels decorated with a chainlike or rope design. Some of the pottery has been carbon-dated to more than 10,000 years, making it the oldest pottery in the world.

Anthropologists do not link the Jomon people to today's Japanese; if anything, they are closer to the northern Ainu people. But excavations of their shell mounds, which contained tuna and whale, as well as coastal fish, indicate a sophisticated settlement of people well adapted to the ocean environment. Such information is relevant insofar as it has a place in the Japanese self-image, especially their notions of uniqueness.

After the Jomon period (c.10,000–300 BCE came the Yayoi (c.300 BCE–300 CE), so called for the wheel-turned pottery produced at this time, but especially significant for the introduction of rice cultivation from the continent. This period saw the settlement of the limited area of flat land between the mountains and the sea. Land shortage and crowding gave rise to the economic use of space that would shape the Japanese way of life. Settled agriculture, and the introduction of bronze and iron, led in turn to the growth of warlike states.

By the fifth century, Japan was divided among numerous clans, of which the largest and most powerful was the Yamato (300-593 CE), based in what is today Nara Prefecture. By now the native

Shinto religion, based on nature worship, had been formalized, and the Japanese imperial dynasty had emerged.

The Impact of Chinese Culture

From the sixth to the eighth centuries, Chinese cultural and political influences entered Japan via Korea and profoundly influenced the Japanese way of life. These influences included Buddhism, the Chinese script, and Chinese methods of government and administration. At a later stage, Confucianism was also imported. Early cities, modeled on the capital of T'ang Dynasty China, were built at Nara (710 CE) and Kyoto (794 CE)—Kyoto remaining the seat of the imperial court until 1868, the year of the Meiji Restoration.

The most famous administrator of this period was Prince Shotoku (573–620 CE), who introduced his Seventeen Articles Constitution, based on the Chinese system of government, and with it a concept of the state; Buddhism was also established as the national religion. Many temples were built in Nara (a short distance from Kyoto) under his direction, some of which, such as the Horyuji, still exist today. By the end of the ninth century, the last Japanese embassy mission to the Chinese imperial court had taken place and the process of "Japanizing" Japan could be said to have begun in earnest. For example, it was during this period that the two phonetic alphabets (kana), which are unique to the Japanese language, were invented.

"Pax Tokugawa"

The adoption of the so-called "Chinese system" of centralized, bureaucratic government, however, was relatively short-lived. From the early twelfth century onward, in an increasingly unstable environment of clan warfare, political power was usurped by military aristocrats, and government was conducted in the name of the Emperor by feudal warriors known as *shogun* (commander-in-chief). Even so, civil war between rival groups was endemic over long periods. This state of anarchy largely came to a halt in October 1600 following the epic battle of Sekigahara, when Tokugawa Ieyasu destroyed most of the opposition and declared himself de facto military ruler of all Japan (reconfirmed by the great battle of Osaka Castle in 1614–15, when the remaining opposition elements of western Japan were eliminated). In 1603 Ieyasu assumed the title of Shogun and set up his Shogunate in Edo.

The outcome, known as the Tokugawa (name of the ruling family) or Edo (now Tokyo) period (1603–1868), was an extraordinary period of sustained peace for over two hundred and fifty years, only ending, after a short-lived civil war, in 1866–67. (The following year, 1868, the Emperor was restored to his historic role as executive head of the nation, moving up from Kyoto to the new capital of Edo—today's Tokyo.) The Edo period was a time of unparalleled economic prosperity and cultural advancement. It witnessed a flowering of the arts, crafts, literature, and general artistry in much of the national life.

It is true that throughout this period society was rigidly stratified and ruled by military families (the feudal lords, or *daimyo*, and their retainers, the *samurai*), but it certainly wasn't feudal in the European sense, as many commentators suggest. Though cut off from the outside world, education, scholarship, and writing flourished; so did organizational skills and technology at certain levels—for example, building techniques and sword- and even gun-making. So that, following the Meiji Restoration of 1868, when Japan moved into a phase of rapid modernization, the infrastructure and human resources were essentially in place to achieve in about thirty years what had taken Great Britain one hundred and fifty. Indeed, within this period Japan defeated both China (in 1894–95) and Russia (in 1904–5) in two major wars, and celebrated her new "imperial world Power" status, as she saw it, in aligning herself with Britain in the historic Anglo-Japanese Alliance of 1902–23.

Western Intervention

In the three-hundred-year period between the mid-1500s and the mid-1800s, there were two key turning points in terms of the West's impact on Japan. The first turning point was in the form of Christianity, brought originally by the Spanish Jesuit missionary St. Francis Xavier during a two-year stay from 1549 to 1551. He and the Jesuits who followed him had considerable success in their proselytizing, making converts among a wide cross-section of the population, including some *daimyo*. There was also the added bonus of trade brought about by the Portuguese merchants who followed

in the wake of the missionaries, and who in turn were followed by Dutch and English merchants. In the 1590s Spanish Franciscan missionaries arrived, who, before long, were arguing with the Portuguese.

This unseemly bickering played into the hands of Japan's political leaders, who saw Christianity as a serious challenge to the status quo. The result was predictable. The warlord Hideyoshi, who had successfully achieved the unification of Japan by 1590, ordered the execution of nine European priests and seventeen native Christians, and announced that Christianity was banned. This was the beginning of the end of Christianity in Japan for over two hundred years. It came to a tragic and terrible halt in 1637–38 when some 37,000 Christian peasants around Nagasaki were slaughtered, following a rebellion over relentless economic and religious oppression.

The second turning point was essentially a response to Japan's withdrawal into total isolation following the expulsion of the Christians. This second event took place between July 1853 and

February 1854 when Commodore Matthew C. Perry of the United States Navy and his squadron of ironclads, "black ships" as the Japanese called them, made two visits to Japan on behalf of the American President to demand a treaty of "trade and amity" with the Japanese. After the July visit Perry made it clear he would be back very soon with an even bigger force and would expect all the documentation in place ready to sign. He returned to Edo (Tokyo) Bay the following February.

Recognizing the sheer might of the American force, and thus of the West as a whole, the Japanese had no choice but to accept the demands. It was agreed that two ports would be open to American ships for fueling and supplies, Shimoda in the south and Hakodate in the north. The "closed door" had finally been pushed open. Within two years the government had signed treaties with England, Russia, and the Netherlands, and other "treaty" ports soon opened. In 1858

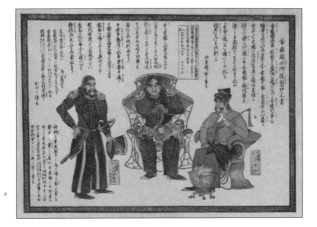

Townsend Harris, the first American consul, negotiated a full commercial treaty, including the unequal provision that Americans would enjoy extraterritoriality (the right to run their own courts) in Japan, as did the other Western nations in due course—a highly contentious issue for the Japanese that was only finally resolved at the end of the century.

As the twentieth century advanced, Japan's endeavors, some would say yearning, to achieve "Western-type nation" recognition—in other words, she did not see herself as an "Asian" nation—were compromised, if not rejected, by the way she was treated in the international arena. This was most obvious at the London Naval Disarmament Conference of 1930, when Japan was told that her navy had to conform to the international limits, based on the perceived status of the different world powers; essentially, Japan was being put in her place. Japanese isolationism was reinforced in 1933, when she walked out of the League of Nations, having refused to give up her view of her rights in China (especially, Manchuria, which she had occupied in 1931, setting up the puppet state of Manchukuo the following year).

This led Japan in the 1930s to rethink her status within her own region, and gradually the idea of an Asian "commonwealth" evolved. Built around the themes of security and prosperity, this would allow Japan access to the materials and markets she desperately needed in an increasingly protectionist world; it resulted in 1940 in the announcement of "the Greater East Asia Co-prosperity Sphere."

There is not the space in this book to delve deeply into history, but it is important to understand the point about perceived and hoped-for Western, "Great Power," status with regard to Japan's entry into the Second World War in December 1941. Although the Japanese Imperial Army was in the ascendancy in the 1930s and indeed throughout the war, and essentially instigated all that happened in Asia and the Pacific (the Imperial Navy's attack on Pearl Harbor, under the command of Admiral Isoroku Yamamoto, was undertaken somewhat reluctantly), it has to be recognized that Japanese national pride, felt at many levels of government, business, and the civil service, had been dealt a blow by the perceived "rejection" of Japan as an equal partner by the West. Not surprisingly, Japan subsequently seized the chance to become master of Asia. After the attack on Pearl Harbor on December 7, 1941 it is reported, although not documented, that Admiral Yamamoto declared: "I fear all we have done today is to awaken a great sleeping giant and fill him with a terrible resolve."

From her defeat by the Allied Powers in August 1945 to the signing of the San Francisco Peace Treaty in September 1951, Japan was administered by the USA Occupation forces. Many liberal and democratic reforms were enacted, and under the new "peace" constitution the power of the Emperor was reduced, sovereignty was formally vested in the people, and Japan renounced her right to go to war in the future (Article 9).

HIROSHIMA AND NAGASAKI

Germany surrendered to the Allied Powers in May 1945; but in the Pacific the Japanese military persisted in fighting on at further great loss of life—especially in the battle for the island of Okinawa (April–June 1945) that resulted in appalling loss of life (some 200,000 Japanese dead, of which 110,000 were military and 75,000 civilians, but there were also thousands of American casualties); Okinawa was the Allies' vital staging post for an invasion of Japan, and the Japanese knew it. Hence the wave after wave of *kamikaze* ("divine wind," or suicide bomber) attacks on the American fleet and what the Japanese saw as a fight to the death.

Meantime, the Japanese government, knowing they were militarily defeated, argued interminably, and failed to reach cabinet consensus on the way forward; so, not unexpectedly, they procrastinated and several times rejected the Potsdam Declaration demanding unconditional surrender, formulated by the Allies in June.

The result was that on the morning of August 6, 1945, an atomic bomb was dropped from a B-29 bomber and exploded approximately 2,000 feet (600 meters) above the city center of Hiroshima, vaporizing everything immediately below it. The only building to survive in any recognizable form was the city's new ferroconcrete Promotion of Industry building, which today is at the center of the Hiroshima Peace Park and Museum.

There was no meaningful response from the Japanese government following the bombing of Hiroshima, so a second bomb was dropped over the old city of Nagasaki on August 9. Because of its historic links to Japan's Christian tradition, the attack—made by a Christian culture—was viewed by some Japanese as perverse and grotesque.

About 200,000 people died in Hiroshima as a direct result of the bomb and the effects of radiation, and 140,000 in Nagasaki. (It is a fact, however, that the loss of life from the Allied fire-bombing of Tokyo and other cities was considerably greater, estimated at nearly three-quarters of a million.) Mercifully, because further atomic bombings were being prepared, on August 14, the Japanese Emperor Hirohito broadcast to his people and asked them to "endure the unendurable"; the next day the Japanese officially accepted the Potsdam Declaration and surrendered unconditionally. On September 2, 1945, the Japanese formally surrendered to General MacArthur on board the battleship USS *Missouri* in Tokyo Bay and the six-year Allied occupation of Japan began.

Reconstruction and Renewal

The program of reconstruction and the virtually free technology transfer that the United States instigated immediately after the end of the war, together with the economic boom that accompanied the Korean War (1950–53), laid the basis for a remarkable period of industrial expansion; by the late 1960s Japan had emerged as the world's third-strongest industrial power after the USA and the USSR, and by the early 1980s she was the second. The "economic miracle" had been accomplished.

Japanese industrial strength has been based on high rates of investment, on the adoption of modern technology, especially robotics, and on the efficient deployment of an industrious and highly skilled workforce. At the same time, her economic success has depended heavily on the use of imported minerals and fuels. Japan is alarmingly deficient in fuel resources, and following the Fukushima nuclear plant disaster in the 2011 earthquake and tsunami which resulted in the closure of all her nuclear plants, now relies on imported crude oil, coal, and liquid gas (LPG) to meet over 90 percent of her energy needs, making Japan the world's biggest importer of LPG. The rest of her energy is produced from electricity which is generated by hydro and oil-fired power stations. Prior to 2011 Japan's nuclear plants produced 32 percent of the country's total energy requirements; currently it is 1 percent, following the reopening of two plants.

The Nuclear Legacy
While the Japanese, as ever, took a pragmatic view of the consequences of war and stoically accepted the enormous loss of life from the atomic bombs and the fire-bombing of their major cities (the historic capital of Kyoto was largely spared by the Allies), surprisingly to some, postwar Japan became the world's first industrialized nation to develop an environmental movement.

There had already been a precedent for such a movement at the end of the nineteenth century, led by Tanaka Shozo, arising out of substantial copper-mine pollution in parts of northern Honshu. Its reemergence in the late 1960s had nothing to do with the nuclear age, but everything to do with the industrial polluting of Japan.

This pollution of air, land, lakes, and rivers—on a scale unknown in the modern world—resulted from Japan's postwar race for growth. Images of face masks and photochemical smog-bound Tokyo and Osaka hit the world's headlines, causing the Japanese enormous loss of face in world opinion. Part of this polluting process involved a number of high-profile and ghastly diseases, affecting mind and body, including "Minamata disease" and "Yokkaichi asthma."

Given Japan's extremely high dependence on imported energy, the Japanese government had had no choice but to sell the need for the establishment of the country's own nuclear power industry (from the mid-1950s onward), and did so successfully, in close cooperation with other nuclear power countries, especially the UK. Pre-Fukushima, Japan had fifty-four nuclear power stations with a target of producing at least 40 percent of the country's electricity generation by 2017.* Clearly, this is now not going to happen given the heightened sensitivities around the nuclear issue. There is no appetite for nuclear arms. Indeed there are right-wing nationalist elements within the country that choose to promote Japan as the "victim" of two nuclear attacks and

* Japan had its own nuclear fusion program and operated a large-scale reprocessing plant and uranium enrichment facility in Amori Prefecture, northern Honshu, to enable the country to have its own complete nuclear fuel cycle.

protests invariably occur whenever nuclear-powered vessels enter Japanese waters. But as noted above, for the most part, Japanese society has moved on. In their own pragmatic way, having turned the entire cataclysmic experience on its head, as it were, the Japanese now see themselves as the catalyst for promoting peace and in the process have become the world's largest donor of humanitarian aid.

The "Bubble" Bursts

The bursting of Japan's so-called "Bubble Economy" at the beginning of the 1990s had a major impact on the economies of Southeast Asia and the United States, her biggest trading partner. Highly inflated land values, huge numbers of "soft" loans underwritten by the banks, high levels of corruption within the insurance, banking, and investment industries, including the penetration of organized crime (see the *Yakuza* on page 94), as well as unsustainable levels of employment all contributed to the "implosion" of the economy.

The Japanese government—raked by factionalism and hampered by constraints resulting from the self-interest of leading politicians, the big business conglomerates, and the highest levels of the bureaucracy, sometimes referred to as the "iron triangle"—failed to achieve a consensus on the basic tenets of reform. It was widely accepted that this process had to begin with the reform of the banking world, including more transparent accounting procedures, to ensure the return of consumer confidence. But since the banks own Japan (the average debt–equity ratio is around 70 percent), and are closely linked to the conglomerates, consensus in this sector was going to be very difficult to achieve.

However, important banking reforms were finally put in place and the economy grew, supported by a surge in exports on the back of an undervalued yen. Then the world financial crisis of 2007–8 hit Japan particularly hard and reversed much of the earlier gains, with the result that by 2009 GDP had contracted by around 5 percent. Japan's so-called "demise" was represented symbolically by Toyota's fall from grace as a result of faulty parts causing accidents in the USA, which in turn triggered law suits and the recall of tens of thousands of vehicles in the US and other major markets. (Even so, Toyota saw a surge in sales in the USA in spring 2010.)

In December 2014, Prime Minister Shinzo Abe, whose Liberal Democratic Party (LDP) had governed Japan for most of the postwar years, called a snap election to consolidate his position with a view to governing Japan for a further four years in order to fully implement his plans (so-called "Abenomics," based on fiscal stimulus, monetary easing, and structural reforms) for reinvigorating the economy and consolidating Japan's position on the world. The turnout was an ambivalent 53 percent, but Abe was successful, securing a significant two-thirds majority in the Lower House. Because of his right-wing tendencies, however, there is concern about Japan's direction of travel in the future. By spring 2016, the Abe agenda looked seriously flawed with little prospect of the third of his "Three Arrows" (structural reform) finding its target, that is, the first two arrows, fiscal stimulus and monetary easing having taken place, sluggish private-sector investment and ongoing labor shortages continue to thwart the Abe enterprise. This, combined with record corporate cash piles that are not being spent on higher wages and capital investment that would stimulate growth, continue to confine the country (probably) to years more of ongoing recession (see Chapter 9).

CHRONOLOGY

c. 10,000–300 BCE   Jomon Period
Characterized by cord-marked pottery.
660 BCE Mythical date of the accession of the first Emperor, Jimmu Tenno.

c. 300 BCE–300 CE   Yayoi Period
Production of elegant pottery with geometric designs and bronze bells decorated with engravings.

c. 300–645 CE   Yamato Period
c. 400 The Yamato clan unifies central Japan.
c. 550 Introduction of Buddhism from Korea.
593–622 Regency of Prince Shotoku.
607 First embassy to China.

710–794   Nara Period
Religious and portrait sculptures made of bronze, clay, or lacquer.
752 Dedication of the Great Buddha (Daibutsu) of Todaiji, Nara.

794–1192   Heian Period
794 Heian becomes the Imperial capital; later called Kyoto.
805 Introduction of the Tendai Buddhist sect.
806 Introduction of the Shingon Buddhist sect.
838 Twelfth and last embassy to China.
858 Fujiwara clan reduces the emperor to a figurehead; central government grows ineffectual; real power in hands of great landowners (*daimyo*).
c.1002–1019 Writing of *Genji Monogatari* (*The Tale of Genji*) by Murasaki Shikibu.

1192–1338   Kamakura Period

1185 Minamoto clan seizes power under Yorimoto, who establishes military rule.

1192 Emperor gives Yorimoto title of *shogun* (commander-in-chief); the shogun rules in the emperor's name.

1274/81 The Mongol Kublai Khan invades Kyushu; ending each time with the destruction of his fleet by a "divinely sent" hurricane, hence *Kamikaze*.

1338–1573   Muromachi Period

1336 Minamoto shogunate overthrown by warlord Takauji Ashikaga, whose shogunate is recognized by the emperor in 1338.

1467–77 Onin War—followed by a hundred years of civil strife.

1542/3 Portuguese sailors land at Tanegashima in Kyushu; followed by Spanish, Dutch, and English traders; introduction of Western firearms.

1549 St. Francis Xavier arrives, begins to preach Roman Catholic faith.

1573–1603   Azuchi-Momoyama Period

1586 Osaka Castle built by warlord Toyotomi Hideyoshi.

1590 Hideyoshi supreme in Japan.

1592 Hideyoshi's first invasion of Korea.

1598 Death of Hideyoshi and withdrawal from Korea.

1600 Victory of warlord Tokugawa Ieyasu at the Battle of Sekigahara.

1603–1868   Edo Period

1603 Title of shogun acquired by Ieyasu.

1614–15 Capture of Osaka Castle, last redoubt of Hideyoshi's heirs.

1622–38 Period of greatest Christian persecutions.

1624 Spanish expelled.

1637–38 Shimabara uprising.

1638 Promulgation of *sakoku-rei* (seclusion) order. All travel forbidden. Foreigners banned, with tightly controlled exceptions.

1639 Portuguese expelled.

1641 Dutch factory moved to Deshima island at the port of Nagasaki.

1673 Opening of Echigoya dry goods store in Edo (evolved into today's Mitsukoshi Department Store).
1811–13 Captivity of Russian Captain Golownin in Hokkaido.
1853 First visit of Commodore Perry at Uraga harbor, Edo Bay.
1854 Second visit of Commodore Perry and signing of Treaty of Kanagawa.
1865 Imperial ratification of treaties with foreign powers.
1866–7 Yoshinobu, fifteenth and last shogun.
1867 Revolt by isolationist nobles overthrows the Tokugawa shogunate.

1868–1912   Meiji Era
1868 Enthronement of Musuhito (Emperor Meiji).
1869 January 3—Charter Oath. Restoration of executive power to Emperor.
1889 Promulgation of the Constitution.
1890 Imperial Rescript on Education.
1894–5 Sino-Japanese War. Japan expels China from Korea.
1899 Revision of the Unequal Treaties.

1902 First Anglo-Japanese Alliance. (Renewed in 1906 and again in 1911.)
1904–5 Russo-Japanese War. Japan drives Russians out of Manchuria and Korea.
1910 Annexation of Korea.

1912–1926   Taisho Era
1914 Japan enters the First World War on side of the Allies; occupies German possessions in the Far East.
1915 "Twenty-one Demands" pressed on China.
1921–22 Washington Conference.
1923 Great Kanto Earthquake
1925 Manhood Suffrage Bill.

1926–1989   Showa Era

1927 Japanese bank crisis.

1929 Wall Street crash.

1930 Signing of London Naval Treaty.

1931 "Manchurian Incident." Japan invades Chinese province of Manchuria and creates puppet state of Manchukuo. Japanese government under control of the military and extreme nationalists.

1933 Japan quits League of Nations.

1937 War resumed with China.

1940 Tripartite Alliance with Germany and Italy. After fall of France, Japan occupies French Indo-China.

1941 7 December: attack on US fleet at Pearl Harbor. USA and Britain declare war on Japan.

1942 Japan conquers Thailand, Burma, Malaya, Dutch East Indies, Philippines, and northern New Guinea.

1945 6 August: Hiroshima atomic bomb; 9 August, Nagasaki atomic bomb. On 14 August Emperor Hirohito broadcasts to nation and accepts unconditional surrender (Potsdam Declaration). Occupation of Japan headed by General Douglas MacArthur, Supreme Commander of the Allied Powers (SCAP).

1946 Framing of "Peace Constitution."

1951 San Francisco Peace Conference.

1952 Occupation of Japan terminated. Full sovereignty regained.

1956 Japan admitted to United Nations.

1964 Tokyo Olympics and opening of Shinkansen—Japan's high-speed rail link between Tokyo and Osaka.

1972 Return of Okinawa (from US administration).

1975 Japan becomes member of G7 group of nations.

1985 Plaza Accord to revalue the yen.

1989–   Heisei Era (Accession of Emperor Akihito)

 2011 Tohoku earthquake

chapter two

VALUES &
ATTITUDES

The Japanese see themselves as a nation apart.
Indeed, the Japanese language itself is unique to
Japan, as is Shinto, its religion. Undoubtedly, some
two hundred and thirty years of isolation from the
rest of the world (1638–1868) have contributed
to this level of national self-consciousness. But
arguably even more important is the fact that
during this same period the Japanese people were

systematically shoe-horned into a culture of conformity by one of the most highly structured and successful oligarchies in history—the Tokugawa Shogunate.

There is a natural inclination in Japan to seek consensus in all aspects of decision-making, combined with the desire to avoid conflict. Underlying this phenomenon is the Japanese ideal of harmony, or *wa*. Historically, the communal effort required for the planting of wet rice, in terms of planning, cooperation, and implementation, is sometimes cited as the key to understanding *wa*.

Unsurprisingly, therefore, we find that Japan is both a "shame" culture and a "face" culture—two sides of the same coin. This is a characteristic shared by the Chinese and other societies in Asia, but it is particularly well defined in Japan. Accordingly, the Japanese have developed a protocol for everything, in business as well as in everyday life, that oils the wheels of social intercourse and insures against loss of face. Here are some examples.

"I" AND "WE"

Because the voice of the group—business, family, school, and social groups—is more important than that of any one individual, Japan is very much a "we" (groupist) culture. In a business context, the Japanese will always refer to their company first and foremost, followed by the name of the department and their personal role within it, and then, lastly, their personal name.

Also, as individuals talking about Japan, Japanese will often use the phrase *ware ware nihonjin*, "we Japanese," thereby distancing themselves from an individual point of view, and expressing instead the view of the whole group, that is, the Japanese people or nation in general.

日本

THE WORK ETHIC

Historically, a heightened sense of the value and importance of work, combined with a goal-orientated work environment, has been commonplace in Japan. It may be that the rice culture and Confucian philosophy have played a part in fostering this attitude over time. It is also very much a matter of pulling together in order to meet goals or targets for the benefit of one's company or enterprise (or institution, or country), and by the same token of not losing face with one's workmates or colleagues.

It goes without saying, however, that the challenges facing Japan today in economic and social terms, including such setbacks as Toyota's engineering flaws, (in 2015 it recalled 6.5 million cars) will inevitably put increasing strain on the resilience of her work ethic; although, having said that, history tells us it is likely to grow stronger, not weaker.

FACE

To lose face—that is, one's dignity, self-respect, or prestige—in any circumstance, wherever one is, is simply not an option in Japan. Whatever it takes, you should avoid creating or allowing situations to arise where loss of face to yourself or a third party could occur. Loss of face is embarrassing; but for the Japanese it is also shameful.

Then, there is the question of personal honor and integrity. Here it is not so much the deed that is necessarily wrong, it is being found out: morality, therefore, in a Western sense is negotiable, and shame is a greater motivation than guilt.

Saving Face

A Danish mayor on an official visit to Tokyo, accompanied by his wife, was invited to play golf by his Japanese hosts. It soon became apparent that his wife was by far the better player. After a while the couple were puzzled by the fact that the mayor's ball, which he invariably hit into the rough, always turned up on the edge of the fairway. The wife's drives were stronger than her husband's, and eventually the Japanese asked if she would mind driving off from the men's tee rather than the women's tee "because it would be more convenient." Rather than have their honored guest lose face by not being good at golf, the Japanese preferred to make sure the mayor's ball was always on the fairway and that his wife didn't have too great an advantage.

HONNE AND *TATEMAI*

Linked to notions of "face" is the distinction the Japanese make of what could be called "public face" (*tatemai*) and "private face" (*honne*). More accurately described, *tatemai* is the façade or even "spin," the gloss put on the presentation of an idea or concept, when true intentions are hidden; whereas *honne* is all to do with actual intentions (thinkof the English word "honest" to help remember the difference). Understanding this somewhat schizophrenic mental environment is vital for all foreigners who have ongoing and long-term relationships with Japanese—whether it is business or personal.

Although relationships develop through a progressive revelation of so-called "private face," it is by no means axiomatic that the Western expectation of "mutuality" in friendships will be forthcoming.

GIRI

This is the highly refined Japanese sense of obligation (or reciprocity) and duty that pervades everyday life at all levels and can never be ignored. It extends to gift-giving and entertainment—choosing a "return meal" in a comparable restaurant, for example. For the Japanese, it even extends to handing money to people in hospital as a contribution to their financial needs; but on leaving the hospital, the individual will be expected to spend up to half the money on a "thank you" gift to the original donor.

HARAGEI

Sometimes referred to as "belly talk" (a literal translation), this term refers to instinctive, gut feelings about a person, event, or proposition. It is often used in a business context about proposed deals and affiliations that are perceived as "right" or "wrong." It is sometimes said that the Japanese will not do business with people they sense to be the "wrong" people, even though the proposition, on the face of it, might be an attractive one.

SUBTLETY, "SOFT TALK," AND "SPACE"

Japan has been described as a culture of pastel rather than primary colors; in other words, concepts and issues tend to fuse into each other and the subtle or indeed "soft" (sometimes "silent"), indirect approach is invariably the best. The Japanese are not loud, in both senses of the word, or confrontational by nature. There is much that is not said but sensed (see *haragei*). Allied to this is the intense feeling of personal and private space.

Thus, when in Japan, don't express affection in public, except to small children, despite the fact that today's youth are much more open in their relationships and in the public way they express themselves. Avoid physical contact at all times, such as slapping backs or holding people by the arm while talking, except perhaps during convivial, all-male drinking sessions. The Japanese tend to keep a greater physical distance from each other when talking, and avoid direct eye contact. Although you might feel uncomfortable, don't move too close.

Pointing to objects or people with your index finger is considered rude. Instead, draw attention by using the whole hand, palm turned upward, in a flowing (not pointing) movement.

The Japanese still prefer bowing to each other on being introduced. To *gaijin* (foreigners), however, they will usually offer their hand, and will probably attempt a combination of handshake and slight bow. The handshake may be light or limp, but don't assume this, along with minimum eye contact, to be a sign of "shiftiness" or "weak character." If no hand is offered, imitate the bow you receive as regards depth and frequency. Keep your arms straight and let the palms slide down your thighs while lowering your torso.

"INSIDE" AND "OUTSIDE'

One of the paradoxes of Japan's apparent "homogeneity" and "consensus" is the extent to which communities great and small are locked into group behavior and group loyalties, and within that into tiers of hierarchies. This groupism (or factionalism if you are referring to politics) is to be found everywhere, creating circles within circles— meaning inevitably that, depending on your position and status, you are always on the inside or the outside of any particular group. This pertains just as much in business. And while you are a member of a particular company, you will also be a member of a particular department, that can, and often does, adopt a position of fierce competitiveness toward other departments.

A helpful analogy might be a comparison between a Japanese person's house and one's own body: the stronger distinction in Japan between what is "inside" and what is "outside" the house makes the point. "Outside" is strange and does not really concern one very much, while "inside" is "intimate" and "cosy," calling for a different kind of behavior.

Inside the house one is greeted by standard home-coming phrases (which in turn are met with standard replies); one changes outdoor shoes in the porch (*genkan*) before entering the house for indoor slippers. Inside, partitionings are often thin, often moveable, and do not screen out sounds from adjacent rooms. Japanese children, therefore, are brought up to tolerate cooperative living in a small space, able to "look away" and "listen away" as required.

One of the most striking aspects of "inside" and "outside" behavior for many first-time visitors is the use or abuse the Japanese make of, say, public transportation. The mess to be found on trains and planes at the end of a journey is testimony to the fact that the train or plane is in "outside" space, if you like, and is treated accordingly.

GIVING THANKS
Effusive thanks for minor matters and incidental help and support are common in Japan. It is always good, therefore, to express your own gratitude more often than you might at home. So, on meeting the person in question again, reinforce your original

appreciation by saying such things as "Thank you for your kindness/help/assistance the other day," regardless of how trivial it may have been.

ETIQUETTE RULES

Remember that in Japanese society etiquette in all its myriad forms, at all levels, is the oil of interpersonal relationships: in other words, there is an acceptable and an unacceptable way of doing everything within the circle(s) in which you are known, as well as expectations of behavior. As an outsider you will not be expected to know all the degrees of subtlety that inform relationships and behavior, but you will be expected to be attentive, respectful, deferential (when required), and project a disposition to show willingness and the desire to learn. Some Western gestures, such as winking or shrugging the shoulders, are not generally known in Japan and may be misunderstood.

ATTITUDES TOWARD FOREIGNERS

There have always been exaggerated observations about Japan's "monolithic homogeneous culture," concerning language, religion, customs, and value-system, as well as her self-image of uniqueness. Nevertheless, compared to other industrialized countries, it has to be said that Japan's declining population of some 126 million is extremely homogeneous, and there is no doubt that, broadly speaking, the Japanese have a very clear sense of national identity. So, of course, do, say, the people of the United States and many European nations, but what is different is the fact that outside the main conurbations of Tokyo, Osaka, Kobe, Nagoya, and so on, it is rare to find any foreigners. Japan, in this and other respects, continues to be a country apart.

In the cities, however, there are substantial numbers of Koreans and Chinese, numbering approximately 500,000 and 655,000 respectively (as of 2014); they are registered separately by the Japanese authorities. Total foreigners numbered just over 2 million, of which citizens from the USA accounted for 51,000 and British 15,000. In addition, Thai, Burmese, Filipino, and Iranian women are to be found in the entertainment districts, and Arab, Pakistani, Indian, and other Asian men are to be found in the odd-job and construction industry—mostly illegal, with the government turning a blind eye.

The strong distinction made in Japan between "inside" and "outside" also pertains to *gaikokujin*, literally "outside country persons," usually abbreviated to *gaijin*. In the old days this may also have included

JAPAN'S "OUTCASTS"

The principal group discriminated against for centuries within Japanese society (today about one percent, or l.4 million, of the population) are known as the *burakumin* or, less acceptably, *eta*—the historic "unclean" underclass associated with the production of leather and other blood-related industries, such as the running of slaughterhouses. Their existence was only officially acknowledged recently, in 1972, when *buraku* issues were mentioned in school textbooks for the first time. Many are associated with the *yakuza,* the criminal underworld, including the Yamaguchi-gumi, Japan's largest crime syndicate.

There have been a number of government initiatives to address their needs, and the problems of discrimination in housing, schooling, and employment. But the Japanese press do not discuss *buraku* issues for fear of reprisals, and there is a significant "non-existent" industry of "private eyes" who undertake the high-risk work of checking the bona fides of Japanese planning marriage to ensure there is no *buraku* blood in either party (when there are doubts); such screening is also undertaken by some employers, and there are "illegal" guidebooks that identify *buraku* communities to assist those planning on moving, etc. When a child is identified as a *burakumin*, school bullying is commonplace. This is one of Japan's "taboo" subjects.

those Japanese not from one's town or province; today, however, it essentially means all non-Japanese.

With their strong emphasis on hierarchy, the Japanese tend to rank foreigners, with "blue-eyed," "white" Americans, Europeans, and Antipodeans at the top, and Koreans generally at the bottom. Visiting Americans, British, Australians and New Zealanders, and Europeans, especially if they speak the highly regarded "world language" of English, can be assured of esteem. But, as so many foreigners who know Japan well will tell you, you are never allowed to forget that you are not Japanese.

INTERNATIONALIZATION

While acknowledging Japan's "difference" in relation to other societies the government continues to project a commitment to "internationalization" (*kokusaika*) which is seen as a highly ambivalent term, and pursued principally through education. The Japan Exchange and Teaching Program (JET), established in 1987, invites English-speaking graduates to act as teaching assistants in Japanese secondary schools and colleges, and local municipal offices (60,000 to date) while in the context of higher education universities are encouraged to accept more foreign students. Whereas, there is little emphasis on sending Japanese students abroad—a prospect that is often seen as suicidal by students fearful of missing out on the job market in Japan and also being tainted with "foreign" values. Such an approach may be seen to support Japan's recognition of a globalized world, but equally, some argue, it does more to preserve Japanese identity.

chapter three

RELIGION, CUSTOMS, & TRADITION

For most Japanese, both Shinto and Bhuddism are embraced together as a normal part of everyday life—with "celebration" events such as the birth of a new child and marriage taking place at a Shinto shrine and the end of life supported by Buddhist funerary rites. At the same time, many Japanese are followers of one of the so-called "new" religions. (See page 61.)

SHINTO

Shinto is an ancient form of nature worship that long predates the arrival of Buddhism in Japan. It was given its name, which translates as "the Way of the Gods," to distinguish it from its later rival from China. The seeking of a harmonious relationship with nature lies at the heart of Shinto. Its many rites, festivals, and popular folk practices are expressions of need, gratitude, and propitiation toward nature. The worship of the Sun Goddess Amaterasu—celebrated at the Grand Shrine of Ise, the holiest place in Japan—together with other hereditary clan ancestors and deities, is part of this broad veneration of the power and mystery of the natural world.

In Shinto all manner of phenomena may embody spiritual energy, or the life force. A waterfall, a mountain crag, a large ancient tree, a peculiarly shaped stone, a bird, or an animal might inspire a sense of awe and wonderment. Such objects of worship and inspiration were called *kami*, a term often translated as spirit, deity, or "god." This is entirely misleading, however, because the *kami* bear no relation to the Judeo-Christian concept of God. It is important to keep this in mind when attempting to understand the so-called "deification" of emperors and soldiers who died for their country. It has been said that to understand Shinto is to understand Japan.

Essentially, there is no ethical content to Shinto, although there is an emphasis on ritual purity that might reflect the Japanese love of bathing and high regard for personal hygiene. The washing of one's hands and mouth is necessary before entering a Shinto shrine. Other than invocations, ceremonial formats, and an assortment of myths and legends, nothing much is written down. Yet a rich array of festivals and ceremonies, especially those connected with rice-planting, harvests, and fertility, take place annually throughout the country, while countless Shinto shrines, each with its characteristic *torii* gateway, adorn the land and mountainscapes.

Torii—the Shinto Shrine Gateway

The *torii* gateway to a Shinto shrine consists of two slanting upright supports and two cross-pieces; it is

THE PRINCIPAL FESTIVALS (*MATSURI*)

There are dozens of festivals held throughout Japan each year, many of ancient Shinto origin. These are a few of the most widely known and celebrated.

Shogatsu
New Year.

Setsubun
3 or 4 February. Traditional beginning of Spring.

Hina Matsuri
3 March. Doll festival for girls.

Tanabata
7 July or 7 August. People write their wishes on strips of paper and attach these to branches of trees or bamboo.

O-bon
15 July. People travel to their hometowns to honor their dead. Festive lanterns are lit to guide the souls of the dead to and from their homes; often floated downriver.

Gion Festival
17 July. Celebrated in Kyoto, famous for its thirty-two floats.

Shichigosan
15 November. Literally "seven, five, three," when girls aged three or seven and boys aged five or seven (usually wearing traditional kimono) are taken to the local Shinto shrine to pray for good health.

usually painted vermilion. Traditionally it was a wooden structure; today replacements are increasingly made of concrete for durability. One of the most spectacular *torii* gateways is to be found at the Itsukushima shrine, rising from the waters of the Inland Sea adjacent to the island of Miyajima.

Japanese shops and family businesses have their own small shrines for the gods of business prosperity, as, often enough, do modern Japanese factories and commercial enterprises.

The deity *Inari* (in the form of a fox) is the most widely worshiped. Traditionally associated with fertility for the rice harvest, he is now seen as the god of good fortune for business. The Japanese home may contain various Shinto talismans and symbols of worship on the *kamidana*, an altar or high shelf for enshrining the household's protective *kami*.

Ema

These are seen at all Shinto shrines. They are inscribed and painted wooden votive tablets, used for interceding with the gods and eliciting favors. They are usually tied on to nearby trees for the gods to notice, and are a favorite way for students to petition the *kami* for success in their exams. The word comes from *e,* meaning picture, and *ma,* meaning horse—an early belief identifying the horse as an intermediary between humans and the gods.

Shinto Ritual

Rituals are mostly conducted by Shinto priests, often with the support of shrine maidens (or *miko*). A Shinto ceremony usually has four aspects: purification, offerings and worship, supplication and prayer, and communion or feast. The process has to do with preparing the participants to communicate with the *kami*; engaging the attention of the *kami*; procedures for placing requests and wishes before the *kami*; and finalizing the procedure through communal feasting. There are other ritual elements, too, such as traditional dancing, intended to entertain the *kami*, performed by the shrine maidens.

For the past fifteen hundred years Shinto ritual has been at the heart of the making of a new Emperor, whose mythical divine descent from Ameratsu reflects the relationship between the *kami*

MEIJI SHRINE

Erected after Emperor Meiji's death in 1912 to enshrine his spirit as a *kami*, (and subsequently that of his wife Empress Shōken who died in 1914) the Meiji shrine in central Tokyo is one of the largest and most visited Shinto shrines, especially during the New Year festival. Meiji ascended the throne in 1868 and reigned during the transformation of Japan into a modern nation state.

YASUKUNI SHRINE

This is the most controversial Shinto shrine in Japan. Located in central Tokyo and opened in 1869, it was founded by Emperor Meiji to commemorate anyone who died in the service of the Japanese Empire. Today, its "Book of Souls" lists some 2,500,000 names, of which 14 are the Class A war criminals convicted by the International Criminal Court at the end of the Second World War. Various Japanese Prime Ministers have visited the shrine (both officially and unofficially), which invariably prompts international outrage.

and the people and land of Japan. This ceremony takes place at the Ise shrine complex on the coast near Nagoya in central Honshu. Following the death of the Emperor Hirohito (reign name "Showa") in 1989, after more than sixty years on the throne, the accession of their new Emperor Akihito (reign name "Heisei") gave the Japanese people, its media and scholars, the first opportunity in generations to examine and discuss the nature of the consecration and enthronement ritual (*Daijosai*). Although this part of the ceremony is entirely hidden from view, the climax appears to be a form of "communion" meal, taken on a bedlike structure known as the *Shinza*

At the center of Japanese culture, therefore, is man's involvement with nature—a relationship that is fundamentally different from Western perceptions. The Western religious tradition regards nature as a mere reflection of the Divine, whereas the Japanese perhaps see in nature the embodiment of the Absolute.

BUDDHISM

Buddhism, which entered Japan via Korea, was an important vehicle for the transmission of Chinese culture from the sixth century onward, when it was adopted by the Yamato court. Following the promulgation in 604 CE of Prince Shotoku's Seventeen Article Constitution, which provided a set of precepts based on Buddhism and on Confucian political and ethical concepts, Buddhism had an enormous and wide-ranging impact on Japan: essentially, it took Japan out of the mists of prehistory and up to the level of an informed, enlightened, and civilized society.

In this earliest period, Buddhism was regarded by the State as a source of both religious and worldly power. As was to be the case twelve hundred years later, prior to and following the Meiji Restoration of 1868, the Japanese rulers of the time chose promising young men to accompany the many embassies to China in order to study the sources of knowledge in all its forms.

With Buddhism came many of the arts and crafts of China. The Buddhist temples built in Japan were themselves amazing architectural masterpieces (such as the Horyuji in Nara), housing beautiful and deeply spiritual bronze, lacquer, or wooden statues of Buddhist divinities, superb religious paintings, and many other works of art. Some of this art came, of course, from China, but increasingly it was produced in Japan.

Buddhism's broad appeal, however, lay not just in its teachings on morality, its ways of attaining spiritual transcendence and enlightenment, or the possibilities of salvation. It lay also in the figures of worship known as buddhas and bodhisattvas—compassionate enlightened beings—that were widely believed to be able to provide worshipers with practical help and support in their lives. It was the appeal of these figures with their supposed magical powers, perhaps seen to be more powerful than the *kami* of the Shinto tradition, that was central to Buddhism's successful entry into Japan.

Buddhism in Japan focused on devotion to the Buddha Amida and his transcendental realm known as Pure Land. Individuals born again into Pure Land attained enlightenment without fail. In the ninth century, two Buddhist schools emerged: the esoteric Shingon "True Word" school founded by Kukai, and the syncretic Tendai school founded by the monk Saicho, and named after a Buddhist holy mountain in China. Both schools successfully accommodated the native Shinto tradition. Both stressed magical incantations, elaborate pictorial representation, and stunning ceremonial, all of which was wonderful for the Japanese aristocrats, but of little use to the common man.

Shamanistic Practices

Still present today, in certain hills and mountains of Japan, are shamans who maintain ancient beliefs and practices relating to "the other world"—a belief system of light and dark, paradise and the underworld—linked to the intervention of *kami* in this world, whose favors to cure sickness and save lost spirits are brought about through dance and trance.

Such practices are sometimes reflected in Japan's so-called "new religious movements" (see page 61), which appeared in the latter part of the twentieth century and can involve trances and the powers to save lost spirits and to heal sicknesses caused by angry ghosts.

In 1175 there was a new development when the monk Honen left the Tendai tradition to embrace the Pure Land teachings. He preached instead an inclusive philosophy, which included the popular concept of salvation through faith, linked to the recitation of certain mantras. It took the name of Jodoshu—*jodo* means "Pure Land" and *shu* means "school" or "sect." His disciples carried his message to all levels of society. Among them was Shinran (1173–1262), who subsequently established Shin (meaning "true") Buddhism in Jodo-shin-shu—"the True Pure Land" school. This was a lay movement with a simple "faith alone" teaching, with parallels to Christianity. Not surprisingly, it has gained converts outside Japan.

Shin Buddhism grew to a point where it dominated all other forms of Buddhism in Japan (including Zen, which was always a minority sect but a greatly influential one within the upper echelons of society), and continues to do so today. There are ten sub-sects of Shin, the biggest by far being Nishi Honganji, the oldest, which traces its highest priest (by lineage) back to Shinran. Not surprisingly, hereditary priesthood is a strong tradition in Shin Buddhism.

NEW RELIGIOUS MOVEMENTS

Japanese religion shows the same capacity to redefine, or repackage, the Great Truths as other belief systems do in the rest of the world. Often enough this comes in the form of new "gurus" who set out their stall, gather their own band of disciples, and then attract a following.

The most notable among the new movements is Soka Gakkai (or "value-creating society"). It teaches a form of "ultimate Buddhism" (that preached by the Tendai monk Nichiren Daishonin, 1222–82), whereby all mankind can achieve eternal peace through renewal, commitment, and dedication to the cause, as well as belief in the potency of the *gohonzon*, "the object of worship," a calligraphic inscription in wood of the mantra "I take refuge in the Lotus of the Wonderful Law Sutra."

Other movements include Tenrikyo, "Religion of the Heavenly Truth," with headquarters in Tenri City, which believes in God the Parent "who created human beings in order that he might share their joy by seeing them lead a joyous life." Mahikari, Seicho-no-le, and Rissho Kosei-kai are others.

Aum Shinrikyo, the sect that instigated the sarin gas attack in the Tokyo subway system in 1993, applied its perverse and warped notions of renewal and purification in this particularly hideous way; the sect continues to be prosecuted.

RELIGION AND THE RITES OF PASSAGE

Among the most important festivals (*matsuri*) and commemorative occasions are the first shrine visit (*hatsumiyamairi*) for new babies, and the *shichigosan* (literally 7–5–3, that is, when boys are five and seven, and girls are three and seven) festival in November for young children. As we have seen, "new beginnings," in fact, are very much part of the Shinto world, when one seeks the blessings of the *kami*; hence the New Year celebrations and the first agricultural activities of the yearly cycle, including the planting of crops, new enterprises, new buildings, and "new starts" generally, including the education cycle.

GION FESTIVAL

The biggest festival (*matsuri*) in Japan is the Gion festival in Kyoto, famous for its spectacular floats—wheeled and portable. The main event takes place on 17 July. It dates back to 869 when the country was overrun by a terrible plague. Gion is one of many summer festivals associated with the eradication of pestilences brought about by the high humidity levels that accompany the hot and very wet weather.

Weddings

A traditional Shinto wedding ceremony is conducted by the priest holding his black mace (*shaku*), dressed in traditional garments (kimono and *hakama*, or divided skirt, often with an outer robe, based on those of the Heian court nobles, and tall ceremonial hat). The priest says prayers and purifies the couple by waving his purification wand (*haraigushi*) over their heads to symbolically sweep away bad spirits and misfortune. The couple also sip *saké* together to mark their union.

After the proceedings, the guests are entertained at a lavish meal, where traditional toasts are made.

It is customary for all guests to bring substantial quantities of folding money (in mint condition), suitably wrapped, as gifts for the couple. Wedding costs in Japan—including the hire of an appropriate venue, mostly in the best hotels—are huge and can severely impoverish the bride's family.

Increasingly, couples also arrange a second "Western-style" wedding—not least because it is exotic and fun (it includes a honeymoon)—in a Christian church or chapel in Japan, or, best of all, in distant places like Hawaii (the number one destination), Guam, Australia, and Europe, which combined account for over 70 percent of all honeymoon destinations.

Western influence has also led to increasing numbers of "marriages for love" replacing the traditional arranged marriage with its use of intermediaries, and accounts for by far the largest number of marriages. Today, partly because of a growing sense of insecurity, the increase in issues concerning loneliness, the disenchantment with "partnering" Web sites and other social media, it is believed that arranged marriages are once again on the increase, accounting perhaps for at least 40 percent of marriages in Japan.

ASPECTS OF TRADITIONAL CULTURE

For the outsider looking in, it is amazing how much of Japan's past exists in the present. This is especially true of traditional cultural pursuits, such as the tea ceremony—perhaps the ultimate expression of Japan's pursuit of pure elegance, as *ikebana* (flower arranging) and calligraphy, arts such as the *noh* and

kabuki theater traditions, crafts such as pottery, lacquerwork, weaving, and dyeing, and pursuits such as the great range of martial arts. We also have to include entertainment such as *sumo* wrestling, as well as Japan's great literary traditions such as writing poetry (*haiku* and *tanka*).

So important has this traditional cultural base been to the Japanese themselves, especially in the rapidly changing, high-tech, postwar world of reconstruction and renewal, that in 1950 the government passed a law known as the Intangible Cultural Properties Act. This honors the top craftsmen in a wide range of designated craft skills with the title "living national treasure" in their lifetime. New names are added regukarly every year, and government stipends are granted to the holders annually to help them improve their techniques and train successors.

One of what might be called the great sub-cultures of Japan—the world of the Samurai, or more romantically *bushido*, "the Way of the Warrior"—has especially enthralled the West, leading to a huge worldwide

following of practitioners in the martial arts, including *kendo* (fencing), *kyudu* (archery), along with *judo*, *aikido*, and *karate* (forms of self-defense without weapons).

chapter four

THE JAPANESE AT HOME

About 60 percent of Japanese homes are owner-occupied. Approximately 34 percent are leased by the private sector, and the remainder are owned by companies or local government for their workers. The percentage of rented accommodation is greater, of course, in the major metropolitan areas. Purchasing your own home in Japan is a dream for many (that is, for those in work), but one that is increasingly difficult to achieve because of high land and building costs. If you work in the main cities, chances are that you will be living in rented accomodation in an apartment block (or *danchi*). If you live in the suburbs, commuting time can be well over an hour each way.

Traditionally, the Japanese house was built of wood and thatch, with sliding inner doors covered in paper, sliding windows with shutters, and deep, overhanging eaves for protection against rain and snow as well as the heat. There was little furniture; some *tansu* (beautifully made portable chests), but no such things as beds or chairs. The floors of the main room were covered in *tatami* (rice straw) mats, with cushions for squatting on at low tables. At night, thick mattresses (*futon*) and bedding were brought out from wall cupboards and spread on the floor for sleeping. Thus one room served as dining-room, sitting-room, and bedroom.

The modern two-story house is still built of timber (with light rendering over timber panels), not least for safety in case of earthquakes, but also because of cost. Tiled roofs have replaced thatch. Most families, even those living in apartment blocks, keep one room as a *tatami* room to maintain their links with tradition; this room will include sliding doors and a *tokonoma*—an alcove featuring a small stripped and polished tree-trunk rising from floor to ceiling, or a side of a larger one (linking in with past building traditions), plus a hanging picture scroll, and *ikebana* (flowers) carefully positioned on the floor.

In some traditional-style rooms there is a recess in the floor directly below the low table, deep enough for your legs; in winter the recess contains a heater (*kotatsu*). (This used to be charcoal fired and was the cause of many house fires; now it is electric.) Sometimes the cushions are formed with arms so that you can relax as you would in a chair.

In contrast, all the other rooms of the house will contain Western-style furniture in the reception rooms and bedrooms, with major household appliances, rice-cooker, and a variety of labor-saving devices in the kitchen, and in the sitting-room and bedrooms, especially those of the children, the latest in computer games and home entertainment. In the family home the television tends to remain on in the background throughout the day.

VISITING A JAPANESE HOME

As a businessman it will be a rare event to enter your host's home, and it is as well to know why not. The average Japanese home is much smaller than in the West and is rarely open to non-kin; entertaining, even within the family, usually takes place outside the home; the housewife is invariably concerned that her conversational English is poor or nonexistent, which is usually the case; there is a further worry that a foreigner will not be familiar with Japanese customs, such as sitting on *tatami*, using the squat-type toilet, eating Japanese food, and so on; and the chances are that the house is in a distant location in the suburbs, making it difficult for the visitor to return to his or her hotel in the evening.

Arrangements to visit a Japanese home can be made through a number of "homestay" organizations. The local Tourist Information Center (TIC) will provide the details. It is also worth approaching the Japanese Embassy prior to departure. In fact, more and more Japanese families are registering as "host families," particularly in connection with the JET graduate teaching program that has now been successfully running in Japan for over twenty years.

REMEMBER THE FOLLOWING

- On entering the house, remove your shoes in the lobby (*genkan*) before stepping up to the house proper. Slippers are provided in the *genkan*, although they may be too small for your feet.

- Before entering any room laid out with *tatami* mats, leave the slippers behind and proceed in stockinged feet. (When you see how finely woven and finished a *tatami* mat is you will understand why shoes are not a good idea. You will also understand why it is important to wear clean socks at all times in case you have to enter a *tatami* room.)

- The traditional Japanese sitting posture for relaxation, squatting on one's legs, can become excruciatingly painful for those not used to it (and that includes many young Japanese today). If a man, therefore, you can sit cross-legged, but women (unless wearing jeans or trousers) should fold their legs under their bodies and move from side to side for comfort.

- On or before entering the toilet, look out for the special slippers—often marked "WC"— and change into these. Don't forget to change back, of course, on leaving the toilet!

THE JAPANESE BATH

The *o-furo*, or bath (never in the same room as the WC), is one of those quintessential Japanese experiences awaiting the visitor. First of all, it is not a bath in the Western sense of a means of cleaning yourself, because that is done outside the tub. Secondly, as you might expect, it is small and compact, but very deep. Thirdly, the water is exceedingly hot—hot enough, in fact, to enable the whole family (typically two parents and two children) to take turns, beginning with the father/husband, enjoying it. (In former times, this could have included the extended family.)

As the honored guest, therefore, the visitor would be the first to use it—at its hottest. The process of stepping into it and, almost without moving, slipping down to sit on the bottom, is a challenging one, to say the least. But it should be experienced—as should any opportunity to visit one of the country's volcanic spas, where the etiquette is the same.

Using the Japanese Bathroom

Undress in the antechamber and place your clothes in one of the baskets provided. Pick up a small towel and enter the bathroom. If others are present, use it to cover your nakedness a little.

Get a washing bowl and soap and squat down on the small stool provided. Then scoop some water from the bath tub, soap your body, and clean yourself all over using the towel. Ladle more water over yourself, taking care not to let any soap spill into the bath. (The Japanese tend to spend considerably more time cleaning themselves than the average Westerner.)

THE O-FURO "EXPERIENCE"

Of course, it is not essential that you get into the tub at all; but if you want to try it, here are some vital guidelines:

- First of all, attempt to cool down a little by soaking your towel under the cold tap and then putting the dripping towel on top of your head.
- Next, step in and submerge yourself up to your neck as quickly as possible; then sit quite still.
- After a few agonizing seconds the pain will subside a little.
- It is essential to remain totally immobile; if you stay in this position long enough you could well begin to enjoy it.
- Once you are comfortable, there is no hurry to get out. The Japanese use the bath both as a source of warmth and relaxation.
- After leaving the tub, wring out the towel and dry yourself with it; this works surprisingly well. If provided, put the cotton *yukata* over your underwear.*

Using the Japanese Toilet

The Japanese-style toilet requires the squat position. For most Westerners this isn't that comfortable, but it is hygienic. Note that the water container servicing the toilet (which one faces on squatting) includes a faucet for washing one's

* Be sure to wrap the left side over the right, which is customary for both sexes. (The opposite wrap is used for the deceased.) Worn with a sash (*obi*), the *yukata* is provided in all hotels. It serves both as a dressing gown and as a nightgown, although it can be difficult to sleep with one on.

hands—the used water draining back into the cistern. The lever hanging down can be pushed left or right, so that either all the water is released or just a small amount. Toilet paper is provided.

Sometimes, the toilet door cannot be locked. The Japanese determine whether or not it is vacant by knocking gently on the outside and then waiting for a counter-knock. It has been known for some Westerners, once inside, to use their body weight to secure their privacy. The problem with this maneuver is that the person on the outside might think the door is stuck . . . .

DECLINE OF THE EXTENDED FAMILY

It was once commonplace in Japan for parents and married children to live together, or at least near enough "for the soup to stay hot" (that is, over the distance between their two properties). But increasingly this is no longer the case, because of limited space in overcrowded apartments, because of relocation caused by shifting patterns of work and employment, or because there is less inclination to do so.

This development very much impinges on Japan's peculiarly large problem of the "aging of the population" following the spectacular postwar baby boom. As life expectancy has soared: 86.3 for women (the highest in the world) and 80.5 for men (third in the world) and a low (but slightly improving) birthrate of 1.43 children per married couple), the problem of managing old age has grown and is expected to become ever more challenging with nearly one-third of the population already over the age of 65 (as at 2015), with the percentage expected to rise to 40 percent by 2050, according to the National Institute of Population. Such a major demographic change brings with it a huge array of attendant problems, not least the management of the economy with the productive-age population dropping to around 60 percent (from 68 percent at the end of the 1970s).

CHILDREN AND FAMILY LIFE

The erosion of traditional family living patterns, ways of life, and value systems (not least because of the impact of Japan's "throwaway culture," where consumption—in the pursuit of being "modern"— was considered a virtue for so long) coincides with a growing problem of youth behavior and discipline, at home, in public, and at school where bullying, for example, has become a major social issue. However, it is important not to exaggerate Japan's predicament, and also to recognize that

other "newly enriched" societies in the postwar industrialized world have encountered similar problems, fed by the culture of "instant gratification" made possible by the new technologies and greatly increased levels of disposable income (pocket money).

Furthermore, Japan so far has not had to cope with the outcomes of the rocketing levels of divorce found in the West, the subsequent impact of broken homes, or the phenomenon of step-families. But the "collective ideal" or "groupism," in which an acceptance of stoicism is central to the pursuit of the "communal greater good," is being increasingly challenged by Young Japan. The search for individuality and individual fulfilment is today more widely expressed in everyday speech and actions, and through the arts, than ever before.

Despite all this, the mother of the family continues to be the dominant factor in a child's upbringing, responsible for supervising her children's education and for managing the family budget. And despite the impact of recession and Japan's poorly performing economy since the early 1990s, especially the breakdown of the "lifetime employment" policy practiced by big companies, with the inevitable increase in levels of unemployment, the Japanese home continues to see very little of the father of the house, who leaves early and returns late. Recent surveys, however, suggest that the modern Japanese married man is spending more time assisting with daily chores, including helping with the children, minimal though this might be in a Western sense.

Although Japan has a five-day working week, Saturdays often involve individual sporting pursuits with colleagues, or some other business commitment, so there is really only one family day each week and that is Sunday, sometimes referred to as "family service day."

It should also be emphazised how important the women's (often hidden) role is in Japanese society.and how misunderstood this is outside Japan. Certainly, they hold the "power" within the family, determining decisions about schooling, behavior and budget , but also in critical roles within the community as carers and contributors to local needs and welfare issues.

Today, however, a new dynamic is in play: with a view to boosting the depleting workforce, Prime Minister Abe's "womanomics" might also be cited here. This is an attempt to encourage Japan's highly discriminatory male-dominated business culture to re-employ women after their families have grown up. Hitherto, it has proved an intractable problem.

chapter five

TIME OUT

THE PURSUIT OF LEISURE

It wasn't that long ago in Japan, certainly
into the mid-1980s, when notions of "leisure" and
"leisure pursuits" were pretty much confined to
the well-to-do or celebrities; it was almost an alien
concept. Spending time on the local golf driving
range, playing *pachinko* (pinball), going to the
cinema, eating out, or jogging were not a "leisure"
thing: they had to do with recreation, improving
your health, or your handicap.

Yet, today, thirty years later, the "world of
leisure" is as much a part of everyday life in Japan
as it is in any other advanced industrialized nation,
now augmented by the phenomenal rise of video
gaming, new technology interests, and *anime*. In
some respects, despite their limited holiday time,
the Japanese are even more committed to the
pursuit of leisure than Westerners because they
approach it, as they tend to do other activities
generally, in a more systematic, structured way,
and this is reinforced by peer group pressure to
imitate. The Japanese also seem to have an innate
passion for what is new, and relish the prospect of
change (as in being "modern") when it is perceived
as "a good thing," whether it be Chinese culture
in the seventh century or American culture in the

twentieth and twenty-first centuries. Curiously, Japan's "No.1 pastime" is *pachinko*—possibly the most intense solitary pursuit ever invented. Located in "parlors" throughout Japan, apart from the entertainment value, they also represent a form of gambling and offer a wide array of prizes which can be exchanged for cash in exchange booths outside the parlor, given that gambling for cash is actually illegal in Japan.

True to form—whereby, to exaggerate a little, everything in Japan that can be documented is recorded, monitored, and assessed—there is a national Leisure Development Center. (The Japanese must be world leaders at data processing.) According to one of its surveys, the year 1995 was a turning point, when a greater number of respondents (35 percent) stated that leisure was more important than work (34 percent). It is worth noting, however, that public opinion surveys in Japan are notoriously unreliable because of the respondents' wish to please the questioner.

The same survey revealed that, in order of preference, the respondents' favorite "free time" pursuits were domestic travel, eating out, excursions by car, and foreign travel. Another very popular pursuit is karaoke which is found in clubs and bars throughout Japan. Indeed, another leisure milestone was reached in 1994, this time with international travel, when a record number of Japanese (11.3 million) traveled overseas. By 2007 the number had grown to over 17 million with China, the United States, and Korea the preferred destinations—in that order. Today, according to the Japan National Tourist Office, some 1.5million Japanese travel abroad every month (many on business of course), the main destinations being China, South Korea, Taiwan, Macau, and Hong Kong. In the US, it is Hawaii and Guam, and in Europe the principal destination is France, followed by Spain and Germany.

SOCIAL LIFE

The very modest size of the average Japanese home is certainly a factor, but the remarkable "prepared to please" culture of the Japanese people has historically provided a huge service infrastructure that caters for all needs, at all levels, at all times. So it is no surprise that a few years ago Tokyo boasted more coffee shops than any other city in the world. It is no surprise, too, that the Japanese don't really entertain at home but invariably outside it in "rented space," however private or intimate that space may be.

This intimate "rented space" is highly regarded and cherished, and can be seen in the vast number of small eating places in the downtown districts of metropolitan Japan and in the countless small bars where *mama-san*—the matron owner or manager—looks after her clientele with kindly charm, sometimes with amazing dexterity in terms of "people management," and invariably with professional aplomb. (Over-imbibing is common, especially among a group of business colleagues; on the other hand, because the Japanese metabolic rate differs from that of Westerners, it takes relatively little alcohol to produce intoxication. In fact, traditionally, drunks, children, and foreigners were excused certain social transgressions.)

Family restaurants are also common, and a typical family week includes eating out locally on Sundays, or heading off for a picnic.

The foundations of this service and entertainment industry are overwhelmingly secured by the enormous expense account budgets of Japan's business world, which are nodded through by the tax office as offsets against profits.

GEISHA AND THE WORLD OF ENTERTAINMENT

Historically, the world of the *geisha*, or "professional entertainer"—involving dance, a simple form of juggling, singing, and such, but not sex, unless you were a patron—for those with pockets deep enough to afford the experience, has been misunderstood and misrepresented by foreigners. In part this is because it would be rare today, and even rarer in times past, for a foreigner to be invited to a geisha evening; in part, because it is unlikely that a foreigner would know how to behave at such an occasion. It is also a facet of Japan that continues to be a "world apart," and the Japanese like it that way. Peddling notions of sex orgies always made good copy, but is far from the truth.

Japan's historic geisha houses are to be found in the Gion quarter of the old imperial city of Kyoto. Like the former tradition of trade apprenticeships in the West, the pathway for the *maiko* (geisha in training) to full geisha status is long and arduous, and requires immense commitment and dedication over many years.

The sex trade itself was traditionally centered on the *yoshiwara*, or "pleasure quarter," but today is found in areas known as "soapland"* (so-called because of the practice of using soap with massage), as well as in bars and clubs where hostesses engage their customers in nonsense-talk, and offer flattery and attention with a view to boosting egos and thus the cashflow of the establishment. Discreet ways of gaining other services are often on hand also.

In this connection, it is worth noting that Japanese attitudes to nudity are quite different from those of the West. There is no shame in nakedness,

* Formally called "turko," as in Turkish Bath, but in the 1980s, at the request of the Turkish government, which found the name offensive, the Japanese organized a competition to choose a new name; the winner was "soapland."

which one quickly discovers at the first experience of a (rapidly disappearing) public bathhouse, or at a hot springs resort.

More importantly, unfettered by the boundaries of the Judeo-Christian moral view of the world, the Japanese are at once more naïve and more matter-of-fact in their attitude toward sex and sexuality. The visitor needs to know that in Japan sex is essentially an entertainment commodity and always has been. In addition, the "pastel" aspect of their culture referred to earlier generates a kind of forgiving "elision" where sexual orientations often seem to collide, where gay and lesbian lifestyles have a positive not negative status (the famous all-girl Takarazuka Revue troupe, founded in 1914, is a good example of this), and where provocative sexual innuendo and images in advertising (magazines, TV, and public billboards) are commonplace.

There are paradoxical elements in this as in many other aspects of Japanese culture. The media world also includes *manga*—the long-established cartoon form used for telling stories, especially religious stories, and communicating information (still used by some government ministries today when putting out new guidelines or information). There are, of course, a great number of childrens' comics, as anywhere else in the world; but there are also violent, brutal, and sexually explicit *manga* that,

typically, the traveling "salaryman" will buy at his departure station and bin at his arrival station. It would be unthinkable to take such obscene rubbish home. By the same token, the soft porn magazines, imported from Europe and America, are "finessed" by students and housewives in warehouses before going into circulation; all shots showing pubic hair are blacked out with an indelible felt-tip pen.

LEISURE AND WORK

The average amount of holiday time taken by working Japanese continues to be about two weeks a year, but, traditionally, it is rare for a worker— blue or white collar—to take more than a week off at any one time. The work ethic and group ethos continue to dominate people's expectations of what is right and appropriate in terms of time away from the workplace, together with fears for promotion.

Group solidarity, as noted earlier, is essentially a given in the work environment; it is reinforced all the time by such things as goal-setting, singing the company song, after-hours socializing, and at annual events like the company outing.

Not surprisingly, it was the Japanese who invented karaoke (from *kara*, "empty," and *oke*, which actually means "tub" or "bucket"; how it came to make up the word *karaoke* is a mystery; but *oke* is not short for "orchestra"), which stormed through Japan in the 1980s and continues to be a de rigueur participatory milestone for visiting businessmen. Obviously, it is not the individual's singing ability that counts, but the willingness to

Holiday Etiquette

Japanese workers employed in a Western subsidiary of a Japanese corporation were shocked. Sandra took off for her two-week holiday, saying, "Thank God, I won't have to see this place for another two weeks." They were even more surprised when the holiday postcard arrived. "Having a lovely time! Glad I'm not there! Ha! Ha!" it crowed. The limit was reached when Sandra returned. "Glad to be back? It's terrible," said Sandra as she settled back into her desk.

A Japanese colleague, reflecting on what had taken place, gave his perspective. "In Japan, if we go on holiday, we thank our fellow workers for taking on our work while we are away and apologize to them for the inconvenience. When we get back we thank them again and maybe give them a little present. Sometimes, we even get back from holiday early to catch up on our work."

pick up a microphone and pretend to be a great singer. Above all, it is joining in, having a laugh, and being prepared to make a fool of yourself that counts. For newcomers, it is sensible to refresh any memories of old favorites like "Country Road," "My Way," "I Left My Heart In San Francisco," "Love Me Tender," and so on.

Once everyone has gone through this ritual, the ice is broken and the party can continue at a more intimate level. Incidentally, some of the latest equipment is so sophisticated, it will improve your performance for you!

CULTURAL LIFE

It is remarkable that the country that embraced modernization (and in some respects "Westernization") with such vigor in the late nineteenth century should have sustained its cultural heritage in such breadth and depth. Certainly, as we have seen, both the Shinto and Buddhist traditions provide the bedrock of this continuity, combined with the historical tradition of what might be called "family vocation." Over the centuries, individual families have sustained particular craft skills, whether it be making dolls, or swords, or dyeing cloth; in the arts there have been similar "family lines," such as actors for *kabuki* (a popular form of drama), *noh* (a highly stylized theatrical form using face masks), *bunraku* (puppets), or *kyogen* (comic drama linked to *noh*).

The traditional Japanese art of calligraphy with a brush attracts thousands to a national annual competition; even more attend an annual *haiku* (a seventeen-syllable poetic form) event. Interest in the two-thousand-year-old sport of *sumo* has never been greater, with, seemingly, the majority of the population avid followers of the six major tournaments, each lasting fifteen days, held in Tokyo and elsewhere in Japan each year. Other ancient sports such as *judo*, *kendo* (Japanese fencing), and *kyudo* (Japanese archery) are also very popular.

SPORTS

Modern sports, too, have also grown enormously in the postwar years. Introduced in 1936, baseball today is a national game; it is played throughout the country and has a two-league system—Central and Pacific—each with six teams. Two of the great pinnacles of the sporting year are the spring and fall national high-school baseball tournaments, held at the Hanshin Koshien Stadium in Kyushu. Soccer has also taken root, particularly in the decade or so leading up to the 2002 World Cup, following the establishment of the J. League in 1992, consisting of sixteen teams.

Golf

Golf is altogether on another level. In Japan, it is undoubtedly the "king of sports," the alpha and omega of aspirations for the nation's manhood and the great prize of the business world, which owns, controls, and exploits it. Nowhere else in the world does it cost so much to join—in the unlikely event, for most people, of it being feasible to do so—with joining fees of up to half a million dollars being paid, and annual fees of US$50,000 being commonplace. In a country with barely enough space to live on, it is not surprising that golf is so astronomically expensive.

So, when the statistics tell us that around 18 million Japanese people play golf, we have to remember that although there are over two thousand golf courses in Japan, most "golfers" are limited to playing at one of the thousands of multitier driving ranges located across the country. It is at such ranges, for most people, that the entire golfing experience takes place, and that includes their driving range handicap.

Another national sport in Japan is volleyball, which is immensely popular among women, and confers great kudos on the participant.

Japan is also part of the "marathon" world of annual events and hosts a number of international marathons, including Tokyo and Osaka; it has also fostered the Universiade (university students) games, which it has hosted on several occasions.

Japan's greatest spectator sport is Sumo. All six annual tournaments are televised and attract vast audiences, whereas the best attended sport is baseball. In more recent times, the popularity of soccer and rugby has also grown.

WINING AND DINING
Tea Drinking
One of Japan's great comforts, as in Britain, is tea, *o-cha*, which, also like Britain, is drunk throughout the day. In the world of business it is routinely served

to the visitor as a matter of course and drunk during the meeting. Japanese tea is green; it is served hot without sugar or milk in a teacup without a handle, so it takes a little practice for the beginner to bring the hot cup to the lips without burning them or dropping the vessel. It is best first to make polite attempts to test the temperature around the rim before drinking.

Tea has been central to Japanese culture for centuries—"the way of Tea" (*chanoyu*) and the formalities of the Tea Ceremony, so called, go back many hundreds of years (see pages 109–11). Although perfected within the disciplines of Zen Buddhism, the custom of taking tea in Japan had long been layered into the cultural life of the ruling class. The greatest "tea master" was the monk Rikyu, who in his time (1522–91) practiced the "art of tea" as part of the political dynamic.

Eating Out

If you venture out alone, you may be refused entry into certain Japanese food or drink establishments. As noted earlier, many are "private space" places, like an English club, where newcomers (including Japanese) are required to be "introduced" by regulars. There is also the persistent fear among the Japanese that you probably don't know enough about local food and customs to cope on your own. But if you go with someone who is known, you will be greeted by the chef/owner/waiters with a heartening "*I-r-a-ssh-ai!*"—"Welcome!"

O-SHIBORI—*THE HOT TOWEL*

Before starting the meal you may be handed a
small folded white towel (*o-shibori*), which is
steaming hot in winter and either hot or cold in
summer. (You may well have been introduced to
this delightful custom on your flight to Japan.)

- Take the towel from its sleeve and unfold it.
  Men have the option of first putting it to their
  face (which can be wonderfully refreshing),
  then wiping their hands and arms.
- Women usually wipe their hands only.
- The *o-shibori* can be refolded, and used later
  during the meal to wipe your fingers.

But there are many other places to eat where
the foreigner is welcome. Wonderful to relate, too,
most general restaurants contain a window display
of amazingly realistic plastic made-up meals with
prices; so that, at worst, you can always ask the
waiter to come to the window and point to the
meal you want.

On being invited out to a Japanese restaurant and
asked about your food preferences, it is usually best
to say that anything will be all right (unless you have
specific allergies, which you would need to make
known), since it is the host's responsibility to order.
Unlike Western gourmet culture, where everyone
at the table makes a personal choice—often with
aching indecision or intimidating bravado—in
Japan the tendency is for everyone to follow the
host's choice, preferring not to be different. So, for
you to do likewise is not a sign of indifference or

indecision—it is a signal of your understanding that will bring great relief all round.

Obviously, if there are items of food served to you that you find unpalatable, just leave them untouched and concentrate on the rest. On the other hand, do try and eat all the rice served in your rice bowl, even though with chopsticks the process can be quite challenging. Rice, as it were, is a "sacred staple" and it is thus a mark of respect not to leave any.

If the meal is traditional Japanese food, try to overcome your ignorance of the conventional eating habits by simply observing and imitating those around you. If you are the guest of honor you may have to be seen to start first, but after that "follow the leader." If, however, you choose not to eat Japanese food, there are restaurants throughout metropolitan Japan that serve the "food of the world"; these include some of the best Chinese restaurants outside China. Gourmets will be interested to know that Tokyo has more Michelin-starred restaurants (10) than anywhere else in the world, including Paris!

Typically, the meal starts when everyone bows slightly and says, "*itadakimasu*" ("I humbly receive"), rather like *bon appetit* in French. In Chapter 7 we'll be introduced to Japanese food and wine, and to the use of chopsticks.

THE PUBLIC TRANSPORTATION SYSTEM

Compared with other countries, Japan's transportation system has a very high dependence on railways—measured in passenger-kilometers it is 30 percent, compared with 20 percent in the USA,

and 10 percent in most of Western Europe. (On the other hand, only about 70 percent of Japan's roads are paved, compared with nearly 100 percent in Europe.) The main provider for the railways was Japan National Railways, which was split up in the 1987 privatization program into six regional passenger companies and one freight company, renamed the Japan Railways Group. In addition, there are many other small regional railway companies. Subway systems operate in Tokyo as well as eight other cities, including Osaka and Nagoya.

As a leading industrialized country, therefore, Japan's railway network plays a much bigger part in the way the country functions, and has to be much more finely tuned, than its equivalent would elsewhere. This systematic approach, one of Japan's great strengths, is no better illustrated than on the commuter train network, where individual train doors are clearly marked on station platforms.

The wonderful logic of this is that everyone knows where to stand, and consequently boards the train speedily and efficiently. On the intercity and regional networks this process takes place with a degree of dignity and calm.

On the underground and suburban trains during rush hour, however, the process is assisted by station staff pushing, along with the passengers, in order to squeeze everybody on just before the doors are closed. It is even known for some passengers to run at the bulging crowd, as if in a rugby scrum, in order to get in. Not surprisingly, under these conditions, do not expect to see a younger person standing up for an older one, or for anyone to give way to a pregnant woman.

This intense proximity to fellow travelers has created its own problems, especially the phenomenon of the wandering hand experienced by female travelers, which certainly, at times, is considerably more distasteful than, say, the "bottom pinching" in Italy. Despite efforts by the authorities to deal with this, the practice does persist since it is almost impossible to police.

When the bus or train car is full, it is best to hang on to one of the straps and attempt to doze while standing, especially as there is often no space even for holding a book or paper in front of one's eyes! Frequent announcements over the public address system alert passengers to the name of the next station, and even which side of the train the next station's platform will be. Announcements are in Japanese, except for the *Shinkansen* (the "bullet train," but literally the "new trunk line"), which are also in English. The Shinkansen, first opened

in time for the 1964 Tokyo Olympics, now links up with every major city in Japan. It runs at speeds of 200 mph (320 kmph) is rarely more than half a minute late and is the most reliable network of its kind in the world.

Incidently, as you make your way out of a crowded train (or bus), it is polite to extend a partly outstretched arm in front of you, with palm held vertically, waving the arm up and down and bowing slightly, at the same time saying, "*sumimasen*" ("excuse me") or "*shitsurei shimasu*" ("I am being rude").

Eating and drinking on long-distance trains is well catered for with trolley services, backed up by cleaners with plastic bags clearing up the leftovers, but is frowned on in commuter trains for obvious reasons. Neither is smoking permitted. Smoking is also prohibited on train platforms, although there are some areas, known as *kitsuen-kona*, where smoking is permitted. Many people purchase an *obento* (lunch box) before departure.

"Shoulder Sleepers"

In late-night trains especially, it is quite common for passengers to fall asleep while sitting upright (catnapping is a common Japanese trait and can be observed in a wide variety of contexts, not least at business meetings). As a result, the sleeper tends to slip over to one side, and should someone be sitting next to them, end up coming to rest on their neighbor's shoulder.

This appears to be tolerated by many Japanese as a "simpatico" gesture, for whatever "conditioning" reasons in the past, but obviously can be disturbing for the foreign visitor, depending on their own sense of well-being at the time!

VISITORS AND THE POLICE

There are many police boxes (*koban*) in Japanese cities, manned around the clock, whose policemen know the surrounding area well and are prepared to assist with finding the all-too-commonly elusive neighborhood addresses.

Visitors have no need to fear encounters with the police, provided they do not attempt to bring prohibited drugs (including marijuana) or pornography into the country, and as long as they carry their passport as identification on them at all times. (Never leave your hotel/lodgings without your passport!)

In fact, Japan continues to be one of the safest countries in the world, regardless of the time of day or night, even though in recent years there has been

an erosion of confidence due to the growing number of homeless people as a result of Japan's economic crisis, and the increasing numbers of younger people "with attitude" in parks and public places, which can be unpleasant but is rarely threatening. Street crime is also rare. In fact, it is still true today that in Japan there is a higher chance of your lost property being handed in, instead of stolen, than in any other country in the world.

Yakuza
Yakuza are part of Japan's historic social structure: they are, in fact, highly trained gangsters, famed for their ornate all-body tattoos, flashy limousines, and the missing top of the little finger, which is their hallmark.

They operate within sophisticated networks, and live from extortion rackets such as prostitution and drugs. They are also closely involved in the construction industry and essentially own the world of *pachinko* parlors. Attempts by government agencies and the law to curb their activities invariably prove futile. They crave publicity and are often dressed in slick Western clothes and drive expensive American cars. The Japanese police simply accept their existence and would only get involved if there were a serious "incident."

Fortunately, it is rare for them to bother foreign businessmen or tourists, so you are unlikely ever to come across them; you certainly should keep your distance if you happen to be in an environment where they are operating.

Taboo Topics

If you want to "win friends and influence people" in Japan, do not initiate a conversation on the subject of the *yakuza*: they are not supposed to exist! Similarly, avoid conversations about the merits or otherwise of the Emperor system, Japan's outcasts (*burakumin*), and the Second World War (officially, Japan was a "war victim"). Most Japanese are very sensitive to anything resembling criticism, particularly when it is justified, so it is best avoided!

chapter six

GIFT GIVING

Learning to do as the Tokyoites do has always been good advice, because in Japan, as the gracious heroine in James Clavell's classic novel *Shogun* * points out, there really are only Japanese ways. The good news for the visitor, however, is that the Japanese know how complicated and nuanced these ways often are and, happily, are invariably forgiving toward the foreigner's faltering attempts to comply.

This is very much the case regarding the highly ritualized custom of gift-giving, which tends to cause more headaches and predeparture distress than any other aspect of the visit. It really should not cause so much angst. A gift in Japanese is referred to as *o-miyage*, literally "honorable present" (the "o" is honorific in Japanese), and in the final analysis your efforts to do the right thing will be appreciated by your Japanese hosts.

Essentially, gift giving in Japan is a form of "social lubricant" to smooth social interaction in the widest sense, including reinforcing existing relationships and mutual obligations. All of this has finally to do with

* Based very sketchily on the story of the first Englishman to reach Japan. William Adams, from Gillingham, Kent (renamed John Blackthorn in the novel), was washed ashore as a result of shipwreck in 1600. Although Clavell undertook considerable research of the Edo period to write the book, it does not claim to be a work of scholarship.

nurturing and sustaining the all-important status quo and sense of well-being, be it within a company or organization, a family, or a neighborhood. Clearly, therefore, foreigners are not expected to know about these things, and, in any event, are not really part of this process. Nevertheless, gifts that foreigners make will be appreciated and mostly reciprocated.

Outside close personal and family relationships, a gift's major function is not to do with "I have plenty, so let's share," or, "This is for you as a unique, special individual." Rather, gifts serve as a device for the balancing of obligations, and above all as a continued reminder of the *importance* of the *relationship*.

If you are not sure about what type of gift to give to suit the level and status of the person who is to receive it, and in due course what type of gift to return, seek an insider's view within the company or organization.

On receiving a gift, some Japanese might give you a token return gift of low value. Don't panic—

KEY GUIDELINES FOR GIFT GIVING

- Gifts should always be wrapped. The presentation of a gift, as with so many things in Japan, including food and ritual, is profoundly important. It comes as no surprise to learn, therefore, that gift wrapping itself is a highly regarded art form and widely practiced. Thus, don't hesitate to ask a Japanese friend to wrap a gift you have brought with you, or you can purchase fancy paper and ribbons at stationery shops and department stores. Of course, if you buy a gift locally in Japan, the shop assistant will be delighted to gift wrap your "naked" gift for you.

- A gift once offered cannot be refused, except if it "smells" like a bribe, in which case it should be returned promptly.

- The Japanese usually belittle their gifts when presenting them. The "unworthy" receiver should in turn express reluctance and initially hesitate to accept it. However, this ritualized exchange has only one outcome, which is never in doubt.

- As a foreigner, you need not belittle your gift in quite the same way when presenting it. But neither should you praise it, nor indicate how much trouble or expense you have gone to acquire it, even if asked by your host to obtain it. This would be gauche and cause much embarrassment.

• Be careful not to give too valuable a gift, since equally expensive return presents are expected of the receiver. This process could continue over a period of time, and be burdensome and expensive for both parties.

• Friends and neighbors traditionally exchange gifts twice a year—at the midyear festival of *o-bon* and at year-end, *o-seibo*, but increasingly, the latter imitates the present-giving custom of Christmas.

• If you are invited to visit a private home, it is customary to present your host with a gift *on leaving*, not on arriving as in the West. By all means, apologize for the paucity of the gift, and don't expect more than a simple thank you; to overdo these occasions with added layers of emotion is bad form. Once again, to avoid any embarrassment the gift will be opened after your departure.

• The Japanese traditionally do not open the gift in the presence of the giver. This allows face to be saved if it turns out to be much more (or less) expensive than was assumed to be the case, or is quite inappropriate. However, there may be times when you are urged to open *your* gift, which you should do graciously.

it has nothing to do with you being a foreigner. It is a kind of "receipt" for your gift—the real return gift will come later. Material gifts can also be given for nonmaterial favors. Seek advice, if necessary, to know whether they are regarded as "balancing."

It is a well-known fact that gifts can "make the rounds" and there are plenty of jokes about one of your own gifts finding its way back to you via a circuitous route of exchanges. The fact is that the shops and supermarkets are so well geared to the gift-giving culture, with standard forms of packaging, that the chances are that you will know exactly what is in the package without having to open it, and can therefore put it to one side for a future ritual presentation.

Given the quantity of gifts that could be exchanged over the years, families and individuals sensibly keep a record of gifts received and given in order to avoid the obvious pitfalls of "thoughtless" duplication.

Of course, there are situations when gifts are not reciprocated because they are mutually perceived as simple expressions of gratitude. These would include the gifts pupils give to their teachers, or the gifts shopkeepers give their customers, or the corporate gifts given to visitors at a car factory, for example, or by an airline (in anticipation of your custom).

As a foreigner, there will be times when you receive a gift unexpectedly and have no way of reciprocating. This should not be a matter of concern that sends you into a dizzy spin. Just ensure you leave with full details of the giver. A tasteful card sent in thanks on your return home, perhaps with a copy of the photograph you may have taken at the time, will be much appreciated.

What to Avoid
Avoid groups of objects (for example, coasters, table mats, or miniature liqueurs) that add up to a series of four or nine: these numbers symbolize death or misfortune. Remember, too, that congratulatory presents are wrapped up in red and white; whereas condolence or memorial gifts are wrapped up in black, blue, or green, and white.

BEFORE DEPARTURE
Try to buy a number of gifts in your hometown, ranging from expensive to inexpensive. Small mementos—even picture postcards of your hometown—are appreciated as tokens of kindness shown.

If you come from an historic town or city (or live close enough to one), or one famous for particular products, then purchase a variety of souvenirs to take with you. These will be most useful gifts and are always well received. You would be well advised to rehearse what you will say about such gifts and the historical context to which they are linked. Keep these observations brief and to the point. (The great cathedral cities of England, for example, always have wonderful gift shops in the precincts of the cathedral.)

In a business context, at the top of your gift list could be high-quality whiskey. Buy the boxed bottles

and take the maximum allowed into Japan (currently three). Chivas Regal as well as quality malts are preferred. Napoleon Brandy is also a good, but expensive, choice. High-quality teas, confectionery, and preserves— such as marmalade, appropriately boxed—make excellent gifts, too, especially if you are likely to be introduced to the wives of Japanese businessmen. And if you run out of such gifts, you can invariably restock at a Japanese department store, albeit at considerably inflated prices.

Not as readily available in Japan are branded luxury foodstuffs such as those from upscale stores in London and New York, so gifts made by these suppliers carry additional status. Other suggestions include silk ties and scarves, commemorative coin or stamp sets, and good-quality illustrated books. Cuff links and tie tacks, incidentally, should be avoided since few Japanese men wear them, but commemorative T-shirts could be a good alternative. Since Japanese business inhabits the world of golf, there could be gift options here, although perhaps only a few that are affordable. Duty-free shops in airports from which there is a direct connection with Japan usually stock these boxed gifts. But avoid relying on buying in-flight, since the whiskey bottles tend to be plastic and not boxed.

Given the Japanese preoccupation with gift-giving, which changes into high gear if foreign trips are involved, it will come as no surprise to learn that there are special "overseas" gift shops at the main airports in Japan that allow the traveler to purchase items before departure—and collect them, all suitably gift wrapped, on return—thus dispensing with the bother of buying them while abroad and bringing them back home: this is another wonderful example of the Japanese "systematic approach" to problem-solving!

The Japanese are the world's number one photographers. Indeed, it is virtually unthinkable that any special event should take place without it being photographed. This is especially true of the group photograph taken on overseas trips, which will be a familiar sight to many host countries around the world. Equally, if you take an "event" photograph when in Japan, a mounted copy of it will always be gratefully received by your host on your return (though don't be distressed if it is never acknowledged).

And Remember This . . .
Don't admire excessively some art object or item in your host's house or office—it might be read as a signal that you want it and they may feel obliged to give it to you!

Another aspect of Japanese gift-giving is the custom of giving gifts in times of danger,

distress, and disorder. Gifts (invariably money presented in money "gift" envelopes) are made by friends, family, and neighbors to people in hospital or who have been injured, or to those who have suffered disaster, from fire, flood, or earthquake. The convention is, however, that following recovery and a return to normality the recipient of the gift will be expected to use up to half the cash received in a reciprocal "thank you, all is well" gift.

Such practices reinforce the fundamental interconnectedness of Japanese society, and may well have roots in the Shinto tradition of appeasing of the gods, responsible for such calamities or distress.

Saint Valentine's Day
In recent years, Japan's gift-giving calendar has been augmented by the inclusion of a Japanese version of Saint Valentine's Day. This has become

a sort of chocolate-frenzy day, when girls give gifts of dark chocolate products to the boys of their choice. On "White Day," one month later, boys give white chocolate products to the girls of their choice. In the weeks leading up to these two events, department stores and supermarkets mount fantastic mouthwatering displays of wrapped and unwrapped chocolate products.

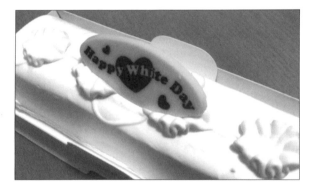

"Domo Arigato"

When presenting a gift in Japan it is the custom to use a particular phrase which implies that what is being given is an insignificant, trifling and worthless thing, when in actual fact it is often far from being "worthless"! Our version which might be "here is a little something" is not dissimilar. Importantly, even though the giver may have little or no English, it is the body language that matters, and simple expression of thanks. "Domo arigato" with a smile of appreciation and slight bow is invariably an appropriate response.

chapter seven

FOOD & DRINK

It is sometimes said that the second-greatest hardship for a Japanese traveling abroad is the absence of, or difficulty in obtaining, *genmaicha*—the brewed green tea and dried rice mixture that is immensely satisfying in smell and taste. In this respect, the Japanese traveler is rather like his English counterpart, who has to tolerate all manner of variations of so-called "tea" that bear little resemblance to his home-brewed "black" tea—made with boiling water and drunk with milk and, for many, sugar. (The greatest hardship for many Japanese traveling abroad is leaving the comforting and reassuring cocoon of their family and work environments.)

The traditional Japanese diet of rice and fish is very different from much of the rest of the world, not least because it has not been influenced by the spice tradition of the neighboring meat-eating countries of Southeast Asia—Japan's main food "enhancers" being limited to the sauces made from soybean and the purée made from the large Japanese radish (*daikon*). Interestingly, many visitors to Japan who have been brought up on a rich carbohydrate-and-meat diet involving a wide variety of heavy gravy mixes and sauces, and who switch to a Japanese diet when in Japan, find that in so doing they experience a cleansing of their own digestive system.

FOOD FOR THOUGHT

To the uninitiated Western palate, a lot of Japanese food tastes rather bland. However, for the Japanese, it is not only the taste that is important: it is the food's consistency when felt with one's tongue inside the mouth, such as that of rice grains and slices of raw fish. Try suspending your judgment at first, as with many things Japanese, and persevere! You may well grow to enjoy judging food by other criteria.

As noted earlier, the Americanization of the Japanese diet has gathered momentum over recent decades, mainly in the increased consumption of meat, especially pork (often in the form of deep-fried cutlets, like schnitzel, known as *tonkatsu*) which is nearly as much as beef and chicken combined), bread, and potatoes, sold through fast-food outlets across metropolitan Japan. The effect of this junk-food element in terms of Japanese youth's expectations of what "eating" and "meals" are is predictable; however, for Japan there has been an additional side effect, namely, the impact of the change of diet, in little more than two generations, on the height and build of the average Japanese child. By 2006, the average height of Japanese men at age nineteen had risen to 5 feet 7½ inches (1.71 meters), and for women of the same age it had risen to 5 feet 2 inches (1.58 meters).

Of course, junk food is by no means the principal cause of growth in stature. Rather it is the result of a significant increase in the consumption of carbohydrates and protein, coming from the postwar habit of eating breakfast cereals with milk, together with toast, bacon, and eggs (although not necessarily together). The Japanese have absorbed these foreign imports so far very successfully—just as they did four centuries ago when the Portuguese introduced new foods, including *tempura* (deep fried fish and vegetables) and a type of cake called *kastera*, found in the Nagasaki region. The daily diet continues to include at least one Japanese meal with rice.

After the Meiji Restoration, another new dish, *sukiyaki* (finely sliced steak cooked with spring onions and other vegetables in an iron pot over a hot flame on the table at which the diners are seated), was introduced in order to encourage the Japanese to eat beef, just like Westerners.

Although beef forms part of the Japanese diet, beef-eating has never really taken off, not least because the price of real beef steak (today, more than ever) is simply unaffordable for most families. Furthermore, up until the late 1800s, meat-eating was seen as incompatible with Buddhist values. Extremely limited grazing land for cattle and the high tariff on imported beef are the principal reasons for the sky-high prices—the highest of all being for Kobe beef, famous for the beer-blowing ceremony prior to slaughter. This involves the cattleman blowing beer in the face of the animals as part of a "calming" process that supposedly helps produce the most tender, mouthwatering steaks.

Dairy farms, of course, have to be near the main conurbations for producing fresh milk; the principal dairy region is the northern island of Hokkaido, which is also Japan's main potato-growing region.

THE TEA CEREMONY

It has been said that to write about Japanese cooking is to enter the world of Japanese aesthetics, philosophy, and way of life. This may be true of all cultures, but it is particularly true of Japan. The embodiment of this notion is the ancient rite of *chanoyu*—the tea ceremony, which can be simply described as an aesthetic pastime unique to Japan that features the serving and drinking of *matcha,* a powdered green tea.

Tea was introduced to Japan from China in the eighth century, but *matcha* did not reach the country until the twelfth century. By the fourteenth century it had become the fashionable drink of the ruling classes—the *samurai, daimyo*, and others in

the upper echelons of society—who would gather in a special place (a *shoin*, or study) to drink it and admire the exquisite works of art, such as paintings and pottery, that had been imported from China.

Gradually, various rules and procedures evolved in the drinking of *matcha*, which were consolidated in the late 1500s by the great Zen monk and tea master Rikyu: in contrast to the ostentation of earlier days, he brought an ascetic and spiritual focus to the occasion, forming the basis of the tea ceremony that is practiced today.

Thus, given its Zen Buddhist roots, the visitor should be aware that *chanoyu* involves a great deal more than drinking a cup of green tea in a stylized manner in a teahouse. According to Zen tradition, the real purpose is to purify the soul by becoming one with Nature—the traditional teahouse (*soan*, or grass hut) being small, rustic, and isolated, with a discreet doorway, as if to reinforce its place in the environment and you within it. Today, as yesterday, the participants are invited to admire the views from the teahouse, as well as the handmade tea-bowls used to take the tea, and any simple artworks that may be on the walls.

What Rikyu Said About Chanoyu

"If one can live in a house whose roof does not leak and can eat enough not to starve, that is sufficient. This is the teaching of Buddha and the spirit of *chanoyu*. One brings water, gathers sticks, boils water, makes tea, and offers it to Buddha. One serves it to others and drinks it himself; this is *chanoyu*."

"BEAUTIFUL" FOOD

The aesthetic factor that informs all Japanese culture, epitomized in *chanoyu*, is certainly very evident in the content, organization, and presentation of Japanese food—to the extent that some Japanese dishes are served with the primary purpose of looking beautiful. There are a number of dishes, such as *tempura* (see below), that are both nutritious and appeal to Westerners, perhaps in part because of their Western (Portuguese) origin. Even so, care will always be taken by the person preparing the food to harmonize food shapes and colors with matching receptacles.

Other popular dishes that appeal to the visitor are *sukiyaki* (as already noted), *yakitori* (grilled chicken), and *teppanyaki* (cubed steak cooked on a hot plate in front of you). Various noodle dishes, such as *udon* (thick white noodle) and *soba*

(brown noodle made from buckwheat), are also very tasty and are served either hot or cold, depending on the season. The most popular noodle is known as *ramen* (typically pork-broth *ramen*); *ramen-ya,* noodle shops, are found throughout Japan. Incidentally, the Japanese take the view that slurping noodles in some way enhances the flavor, so feel free to join in the noodle symphony, as required!

Rice *(gohan)*, of course, is a Japanese staple and is often the major ingredient of the meal. Served in a deep bowl *(domburi)*, it could be topped with broiled eel (which is delicious) or chicken and egg. Eel and rice is called *unagi domburi*, and chicken and egg *o-ya-ko domburi* (literally "parent and child").

An inexpensive dish, popular with Westerners, is *o-konomi-yaki* (literally "your favorite grill"), where you pour batter onto small pieces of beef, pork, prawns, or various vegetables, and prepare it like an omelette on a hotplate in the middle of the table.

FISH DISHES

As you might expect from one of the world's major fishing nations, there are countless Japanese dishes based on food from the sea. If boiled or fried, the taste may be familiar to the Western palate; but when eaten raw (*sashimi*) for the first time, it may be necessary for some (as one writer has put it) to jump over one's own shadow, although, for others, the flesh texture of uncooked fish, dipped in soy source and hot radish purée, will be an entirely positive experience from the outset—whether it is raw tuna, red sea bream, or salmon. (See also page 18.) An easier introduction, perhaps, is to start with *sushi,* which is Japan's most popular fish dish (tiny pieces of raw fish placed on top of rice, with mustard and ginger, often wrapped in thin leaves of seaweed). *Sushi* has actually become one of Japan's most successful food exports thanks to the Western supermarket chains that now sell it, mostly locally produced. However, top quality *sushi* in Japan can be very expensive.

FOOD ETIQUETTE

- Meals in Japan traditionally begin with the phrase "*itadakimasu*" (literally, "I humbly receive," or more colloquially "let's eat"), said in unison. It is similar to "*bon appétit*," or saying grace to give thanks before a meal.

- Take the wooden chopsticks from their paper sleeve, split them, then lay them on the rest provided until the meal arrives. Using your chopsticks, take from the various bowls of food presented to you and eat directly; there is no special eating plate or bowl (except the rice bowl).

- A proper Japanese meal always includes rice. Other dishes are added, depending on how elaborate the meal is.

- Instead of a succession of courses, most Japanese food is served all at once.

- The guest is required to take small portions from each dish without neglecting any.

- Bowls should be lifted in the hand when eating from them.

- It is not good manners to linger too long over any one kind of food. But, of course, as a foreigner, you can leave untouched any dish you don't like.

- Before starting, remove the rice bowl lid and place it upside down on the left. Then do the same with the soup bowl cover, but place this on the right.

- You can lift the bowl containing rice to your mouth with your left hand, for the purpose of eating more efficiently. Naturally, you drink the soup directly from your soup bowl.

- If your rice bowl is empty, ask to have it filled from the large pot. As on all other occasions when giving or receiving something, it is polite to use both hands when lifting the bowl.

- Rice left in your bowl indicates that you want more. To show that you have finished, pick out all the grains with your chopsticks and eat them. In any event, eating all the grains in the rice bowl is considered good manners.

- For dishes from which all guests can help themselves, use the special chopsticks or spoons provided. If absent, reverse your own chopsticks and transfer the food with the clean ends.

- When finished, replace the covers of the bowls, and place the chopsticks side by side onto the rice bowl or on the special wooden or ceramic chopstick rest provided.

- Finally, say "*go-chiso-sama desh'ta*" ("It was a feast," or "Many thanks for the meal") on leaving, and bow slightly.

Japan's principal fish market is Tsukiji in Tokyo, and well worth a visit. So important is freshness, that rail tracks run into Tsukiji market so that trains can speed the fish to destinations all over the country in the shortest possible time.

USING CHOPSTICKS

Mastering the use of chopsticks takes some practice, depending on your dexterity. Try the following steps to help develop your technique.

Wedge the lower chopstick firmly in the crotch of your hand, holding it in place between the base of the thumb and the tip of the ring finger. It must not move!

Then hold the upper chopstick quite independently, like a pen, between the tips of the thumb, index finger, and middle finger.

Practice holding the chopsticks one at a time. Then take both chopsticks and align their tips by pushing them against a flat surface, such as the table top.

Finally, try picking up an object (like a piece of bread, or a cooked bean) by moving the tip of the the upper chopstick onto the stationary lower one.

Once adept at using the chopsticks, remember not to cross them on putting them down; and certainly never (heaven forbid!) to stick them into the rice as a repository!

DRINKING ETIQUETTE

- Whenever alcohol is served, raise your glass or cup to have it filled, and take a sip before putting it down. It is considered good manners to hold the cup or glass with both hands.
- Offer to serve others of your party if they have served you; in principle, one never serves one's own drinks.
- As a sign of esteem and friendship you may be offered another guest's *saké* cup. Accept it with thanks, and raise it to be filled. Later (not immediately) you can offer your cup, after having cleaned it, and pour *saké* in return.
- The Japanese toast for "Your health!" is "*Kampai!*" (literally "a dry cup").
- Beer has now overtaken *saké* as the most common drink drunk with meals, with wine growing in popularity all the time as well. Unless you are at a Western restaurant, you will almost certainly be offered the choice of beer or *saké*.
- Your empty glass or cup signals to your host that you would like it filled; leave the glass or cup full or nearly full, therefore, if you don't want any more to drink.

SOMETHING ABOUT *SAKÉ*

Although *saké* is known as traditional Japanese rice wine—it has an alcohol content, like sherry, of around 15 percent, but this can be higher—in fact it is brewed like beer. Like beer, it is made in many parts of Japan and, for connoisseurs, has distinct regional characteristics. There is also dry, medium, and sweet *saké*, so that you can choose the *saké* to suit the food you are eating.

Drunk on its own, usually from small porcelain cups, *saké* is often taken with a touch of salt on the rim of the cup. It is mostly drunk heated (the *saké* bottle or flask is immersed in hot water) to room or body heat temperature; in the summer it is also

drunk slightly chilled. However, *saké* does not keep as wine does, so there are no "vintage" *sakés* as such. Brewing commences in the fall, after the rice harvest, and the process is completed by the following February. After this, the product is kept still throughout the summer and put on sale the following fall (in October) when it reaches its full maturity.

Saké is also drunk at many formal and celebratory occasions throughout the year, including, as we have seen, the marriage ceremony of *san-san-kudo*, or "three times three" (when the bride and groom each take three sips from the *saké* cup three times, nine sips in all), at burials, when a child is born, at the many *matsuri* (festivals, see page 53), and even at events such as the opening of a new office or the start of a new enterprise. It is no wonder, as one wag has said, that there is barely enough *saké* brewed for a year's needs, never mind any thoughts of "putting some down" for the future. Actually, *saké* does keep, but over a period of time it transmutes into a kind of syrupy nectar.

The Golden Drinking Rule
Never mix *saké* with Western-style spirits, such as cognac or whiskey: the cocktail can be quite lethal, causing nausea, sickness, and rapid dehydration. *Saké* followed by beer during the course of an evening is normally harmless in moderation.

THE JAPANESE COOKERY BASKET

Some of the most common ingredients used in cooking in Japan are as follows:

Aji-no-moto. A widely used seasoning based on monosodium glutamate (invented in Japan) and designed to bring out the food flavors.

Bean curd *(tofu)*. A mild-flavored product made from the pureeing of white soy beans, pressed into cakes and used widely in cooking.

Dried bonito *(katsuobushi)*. This is the basic ingredient of the standard Japanese soup stock. The bonito fish is dried solid so that it can be grated to make the soup.

Ginger *(shoga)*. Grated or sliced and used in soups and sauces.

Horseradish (*wasabi*). Slightly stronger than the European variety, it comes in powdered form or is grated as a garnish for *sashimi* and *sushi*. The radish itself, as already noted, is called *daikon* or "big root."

Noodles (see pages 111–112).

Saké, for seasoning.

Soy sauce *(shoyu)*, the most common of Japanese seasonings. It is available both as a light soy (*usukuchi*) or dark soy (*koikuchi*). Soy sauces in the West, however, are much stronger.

Soy bean paste (*miso*) is used in all types of Japanese dishes. As a soup, it is the traditional Japanese breakfast, and sweetened it forms the most basic Japanese cake.

OBENTO—*THE LUNCH BOX*
Perhaps the most famous Japanese food item of all is the ubiquitous *obento*, or "lunch box." Available throughout Japan, and eaten by schoolchildren and workers alike, it can be found everywhere—on boats, planes, and trains, at every major station, at all supermarkets and local "mom and pop" stores, in street kiosks serving offices: it is the food that feeds Japan, at least at lunchtime. These days the box is made of plastic; it contains an assortment of foods, including noodles, rice, pickles, and cake.

Going for Percentages
There are a number of distilled by-products from rice; one such drink is *shochu*, known as "Japanese white liquor," which is a serious contender for being among the top "fire waters" at 70 percent proof!

SOME LANGUAGE TIPS ON EATING OUT
As we have seen, many ordinary Japanese restaurants display plastic or wax replicas of their meals, with price tags, in their front windows. You

can, therefore, go into a restaurant with a degree of confidence (albeit with no Japanese language skills at this stage), say "*Sumimasen*" ("excuse me") to attract the attention of the waiter or waitress, and then say "*Sho-uindo no yo na,*" which will indicate that you have seen something in the show window that has taken your fancy.

Next, take the waiter or waitress into the street and point at the meal you want, saying "*Are kudasai*" (*are* meaning "that over there") if what you want is away from your pointing finger, or "*Sore kudasai*" ("this here") if what you want is near your finger.

When the meal arrives at your table, say "*go-chiso-sama*" ("What a feast!"). Then, when finished, ask for your bill by saying "*o-kanjo kudasai.*" When paying, repeat "*go-chiso-sama desh'ta*" ("It really was a feast!")

chapter eight

LIVING IN JAPAN

"Internationalization" (*kokusaika*) has been a buzzword in Japan since the 1980s, and a number of high-profile initiatives by the Japanese government have been undertaken to highlight Japan's "connectedness" to the outside world, most notably the JET (Japan Exchange and Teaching) program for graduate students from North America, Australasia, and the UK, who teach English for a year or so in Japanese schools. Also currently in play, as noted earlier, is the new "endeavor" to attract more foreign students to Japanese universities, which regrettably actually only reinforces the Japanese mindset of "separateness". Thus, such endeavors can only be of token value in the great scheme of things. It remains a fact, even as we advance into the second decade of the twenty-first century, and despite the huge level of Western, especially American, influence, that only a tiny proportion of Japanese can actually *speak* English (including teachers of English); that there are still areas of the country that rarely, if ever, see a foreigner; that the vast majority of Japanese have never left Japan; and that as an island nation they are over five times farther away (112 miles) from their nearest neighbor (Korea) than, say, Britain is to hers (20 miles from France at the nearest point).

"EXAMINATION ENGLISH"

The English taught in Japanese schools is essentially literary rather than spoken or practical. Attempts in the past to change this have failed to make any impression at all. Widely known as "examination English," it has nothing to do with conversational skills and everything to do with grammar, vocabulary, and comprehension.

The lack of English-language skills in Japan at all levels is one of the biggest reasons it is failing to gain a strong foothold in international bureaucratic and corporate life, commensurate with its economic and industrial status. For example, Japan does not have a single business school in the global top 100 and its number one business school, Keio, continues to conduct education and management programs in Japanese.

Of those Japanese who have traveled overseas, many will have been in tour groups, for a very short period of time—days rather than weeks. They will have flown in a Japanese airline, and may well have stayed in Japanese hotels and eaten Japanese food throughout the period away. They will have taken innumerable photographs, but will not have much of an idea of what they saw or its significance. They will not have spoken to a single foreigner, or attempted to do so, because they are without the necessary spoken language skills. Thus, the "overseas" trip will virtually have taken place within a hermetically sealed Japanese environment.

REJECTING THE RETURNEE

Japanese children who have lived overseas with their parents, because of job assignments, can and often do experience great difficulty in reintegrating with their peers and with society in general. Apart from the inevitable difficulties in dealing with the curriculum, the problem stems from the fact that they are perceived to be partly "foreign" or "outside," because they have spent some of their life in another culture. The response to this perception in its worst form can be bullying. Consequently, special "reorientation schools" have grown up to deal with the increasing numbers of children who fall into this category. Of course, in the long term, such children should provide a wonderful, skilled resource for Japan and her international needs; but given the conformist strictures within Japanese society, it is unlikely that such a resource will be recognized (other than by foreigners!).

This notion of connectedness—or perhaps, more accurately, non-connectedness—is especially well illustrated in a typical homecoming celebration for a Japanese businessman, returning from a two- or three-year overseas assignment. The context might strike some as not dissimilar to the family jubilation on the return of the prodigal son. It would not be unusual for the welcoming colleagues, friends, and family largely to ignore the overseas experience of the returnee and to concentrate entirely on bringing him up to date on the "real world," that is, Japan, which, mercifully, he has once again been able to embrace.

The key to living in Japan, therefore, lies, first of all, in understanding this sense of separateness and difference, and second, in observing the golden rule "to do as the Tokyoites do." The following figures show the numbers of foreigners (*gaijin*) living/ working in Japan. It is a sign of the times that the largest foreign group in Japan is now Chinese.

JAPAN'S FOREIGN RESIDENTS BY COUNTRY (2014)	
Total 2,121,831 [approx. 1.6% of total population	
China	654,777
Korea	501,230
Philippines	217,585
Brazil	175,410
Vietnam	99,865
United States	51,256
Peru	47,978
Thailand	43,081
Indonesia	30,210
United Kingdom	15,262
Australia	9,350
France	9,461
Russia	7,859
SOURCE: Japanese Ministry of Justice, 2016	

Visitors should know that the Koreans, for the historic reasons of annexation (1910–45) and their involvement, military and civilian, at so many levels in the Second World War, are treated as a separate group. There is a reminder of this on arrival in Japan at passport control, which requires Koreans to go through a separate channel. All other peoples from the rest of the world are referred to as "Non-Japanese."

On arrival, it is sensible and good manners to respect Japanese regulations on what can and cannot be brought into the country. Japanese customs officials are usually polite, persistent, and very thorough; for example, if you have brought more than your quota of whiskey or other alchoholic beverages or cigarettes (three 3 oz or 75 ml bottles and 400 cigarettes respectively) it is best to say so before being challenged. You will be charged duty. However, if you attempt to bring in drugs or pornography, the reception will be far from cordial.

Your first airport in Japan is likely to be Narita, some 37 miles (60 kilometers) outside Tokyo in Chiba prefecture. Originally planned in the 1960s, before Japan became a world player and before the age of Boeing 747s, it was built on valuable farmland, and such was the environmental outcry over the plans that it took years of litigation to move the scheme forward. (When the airport finally opened in 1977, parts of it were still being cultivated by owner farmers who had not yet agreed a settlement!) Narita finally opened a second shorter runway for smaller budget aircraft in 2002 against huge opposition from adjacent landowners. Construction of a third runway is still under discussion.

The journey to Tokyo can take over two hours by road. Unless you are being met by a company/host limousine, the simplest and fastest option is to take the Narita Express straight to Tokyo Station (one hour).

Meanwhile, Haneda, Tokyo's original airport located only 8 miles from Tokyo once seen as Japan's "domestic" hub, is now gaining increasing numbers of international (regional) flights and is seen by the government as a vital option for supporting Tokyo's Olympic Games in 2020.

"FINDING YOUR WAY"

There is much that is contradictory (in Western terms) in Japan and even illogical. It is something all visitors, whoever they are, have to come to terms with. One such instance is street names and numbers, or, rather, the lack of them. Partly because of poor planning laws, and the consequent haphazard development of towns and cities, street names and numbers are either a jumble or don't exist. Going from A to B in metropolitan Japan, therefore, can be one of the most challenging and frustrating things you do!

So, unless you know the particular building or house you are visiting, locating an address in Japan should be regarded more as an endurance test than a matter of routine. Hotels are generally good at writing down directions for the taxi driver (usually involving simplified map drawings), but failing that, even though you may have been given landmarks (" . . . two streets up from left of the Daiwa Building . . .") to help you locate the spot, the visitor may well end up having to plead for help at the nearest *koban* (police box), which of course you also need to find, and provide the on-duty police officer, (who probably doesn't speak English) with as much information as possible. It is also reassuring to know that because of the complexity of the street system the Japanese themselves are invariably sympathetic to enquiries, as long as you are able to make yourself understood. (Ideally, ask your interlocutor to draw a simplified map for you with clear signs of where you go next; otherwise, unless you have the language skills, you won't understand the directions!)

"IN JAPAN, NOTHING CHANGES"

Old hands meeting new hands who are about to spend some time in Japan tend to want to "preach the gospel" to the new arrivals—their first lesson being that it is important to understand one fundamental fact of life, namely, that in Japan "nothing changes." This is essentially shorthand for saying that Japan is built by and for the Japanese, and that any beneficial change (especially for foreigners), whether it be dealing with landlords, the local tax office, tradesmen, a complaint to the municipal offices, or whatever, is essentially glacial—that is, slow to the point of being imperceptible (or even nonexistent!).

As this guide has tried to show, while recognizing that in Japan there are only Japanese ways, there are also huge benefits to be gained by caring and sharing; using your best instincts in applying deference, consideration, and some humility in the processes of problem-solving and developing relationships will bring their own reward. The Japanese approach to relationships and the workings of *haragei* (gut instinct) are part of a process that is always looking to the longer term. Nevertheless, you can often get good tips from Western businessmen with a wealth of experience in Japan that will be of practical value.

ENTRY REQUIREMENTS

You will have already addressed these matters using other sources, but it may be useful here to be reminded that visitors from the United States, Canada, and New Zealand are limited to a ninety-day (nonworking) visa. Visitors from Britain and Ireland do not require visas for nonworking visits of less than 180 days, although on arrival you are likely to be granted an initial, extendible, stay of ninety days only. Visa renewal may well require you to leave the country (to, say, Korea or Hong Kong) and reenter. There are special six-month, extendible, working-holiday visas available for young people aged between eighteen to twenty-five from Australia, New Zealand, and Canada.

For stays of any kind longer than ninety days, an Alien Registration Card (ARC) is mandatory, obtainable from the Municipality Ward Office (MWO) where you reside, and which you are required to carry with you at all times. At the MWO, by the way, you will be fingerprinted; this has been a highly contentious issue for years, but it remains part of the "due process" for foreign residents.

But be aware that if you need to leave Japan, for business or holiday reasons, you are required to obtain a reentry permit before your departure. Failure to do so will involve cancellation of your Alien Registration Certificate and you will have to go through the whole registration procedure again!

Also, be aware of Japan's new requirement for fingerprinting foreigners, introduced in 2007 as an anti-terrorist measure. However, the regulation excludes "special" foreign residents, namely those of Chinese and Korean descent, because of historical sensitivities. Also exempt are diplomats and children under sixteen.

SOME "HOUSEKEEPING" INFORMATION

Electricity Domestic electricity supply throughout Japan is 100 volts AC, although modern houses and flats are more likely to have 200 volts, which is essential to run power appliances such as air-conditioning or central heating units.

Time There is no "summer time" in Japan so the clocks do not change. Japan Standard Time is GMT + 9 hours in the UK, - 5 hours in New York, and + 10 hours in Sydney.

DRIVING IN JAPAN

You cannot buy a car in Japan unless you can demonstrate that you have a big enough parking space for it. Once you see the maze of narrow, interlinking streets in metropolitan Japan, you will quickly appreciate why off-street parking is mandatory. So dealers are unable to sell you a car without evidence that you have somewhere legal to park it! (The transaction involves an official form of clearance issued by the police.)

Driving is on the left, and motorways operate a toll system, with costs fixed according to the distances traveled. The roads are numbered, which makes it relatively easy to follow a route without trying to decipher the Japanese characters (in *kanji*) on the signboards. Spot checks by police are common—so never drive without your papers and license to hand over—and the drunk-driving laws are rigorously enforced. The average traveling speed in central Tokyo can be as low as 8 mph; taxis tend to rule the roost there and will dart about, crossing lanes and making sudden turns that test the nerve of even the most skilled visiting driver.

The Japanese Calendar Date stamping on all official documents in Japan is unique and is based on the reign of the current Emperor. Thus, on the accession of a new Emperor, the era is given a name (currently *Heisei*) and the calendar reverts to year 1. The order for writing the date is year/month/day. This official form of dating will be found throughout Japan, from banks and post offices to municipal offices and stores.

Measurement Japan uses the metric system.

Animals Japan is an animal-friendly country and it is relatively easy to "import" pets; cats need no documents, but dogs need two, and there are annual procedures to follow once in the country. (Never forget that Japan is a country of "procedures"!)

Accommodation Apart from the "Western-style" apartments, which tend to be very expensive, there are those that mix Japanese and Western style and can be pleasant enough. Typically, there will be one *tatami* room, while the others will have carpets or wooden floors. The bathroom will invariably be the Japanese type—a unit complete with shower and an independent heater for the bathtub itself—and there will probably be a Japanese-style toilet. All apartments have a small entrance hall (*genkan*) where you take off your shoes before entering.

Room Size Japanese rooms are measured according to the number of *tatami* mats required to cover the floor space. A mat is approximately 2.4 square yards (2 x 1 meters), so a six-mat room is 14.4 square yards (12 square meters).

Garbage Collection Collections in metropolitan Japan take place frequently—up to four times a week in Tokyo, for example—but the garbage has to be separated before collection into bags of burnable and nonburnable material. There are specified days and times for these collections. There is also a collection day for large items, such as unwanted furniture; printed matter is also collected separately.

Insurance Provision of insurance by all insurance companies, domestic and foreign, is strictly regulated by the Ministry of Finance, so that coverage and pricing is effectively uniform. All insurance transactions, of course, are in Japanese, but the international companies represented in Japan can handle most requirements.

Health Because of the high cost of medical treatment in Japan, it is essential to take out medical insurance. Most foreigners tend to turn to the many private clinics for treatment as required, but it is possible to join Japan's National Health Scheme (*Kokumin Kenko Hoken*). However, this does not necessarily provide 100 percent coverage and is not always accepted by the clinics. Furthermore, Japan's NHS is by no means a paragon of state-supplied healthcare, and if a patient is hospitalized his or her family is expected to lend a hand in the nursing care.

Doctors and Medicines Most physicians in Japan are specialists, but there are plenty of highly trained doctors serving the foreign community. (Embassies have lists of these doctors.) Should you be taken ill in one of Japan's many international hotels, for example, there will be an English-speaking doctor on call to attend to you. Incidentally, if you take a prescription with you to Japan, it will not be accepted; it will need to be rewritten by a local practitioner. Rest assured, however, that Japan maintains very high standards in the medical field, and Japanese pharmaceutical products are of the highest quality. Medicines are dispensed at hospitals and clinics where medical treatment is provided, and at drug stores where a prescription can be made up.

The Police Soon after moving in you will almost certainly be visited by a police officer from your local *koban* (police box); you will be asked to

complete a simple form giving details about yourself. This is not a "Big Brother" imposition and may well be useful in an emergency.

Food and Water Drinking water is safe throughout Japan and the standard of fresh food is universally very high.

EVERYDAY LIFE

One of the first things you will find yourself doing on arrival in Japan is bowing—almost automatically. The Japanese do not shake hands (except in Western-style contexts) but bow by way of acknowledgment and greeting at all times. You will find elevator attendants in hotels bowing as you enter the elevator, attendants in department stores bowing as you step on to the escalator, and the platform attendant bowing as the train leaves the station. You will even see people bowing when making a telephone call.

There is a bowing etiquette and hierarchy as between older and younger, junior and senior in rank, determining how much bowing should be done and the depth of the bow; indeed, you will often see the elderly bowing endlessly at times. But it is surprising how easily the bowing routine is acquired and the foreigner should not be concerned about the finer points of this aspect of manners; it is the gesture that counts.

An important aspect of everyday life is the male-female role and the expectations surrounding it. It is worth considering this at all times on "social" occasions. Japanese couples, for example, especially

---

CALLING ON A JAPANESE FAMILY

It is an honor to be invited to a private house in Japan. On arrival, you might be introduced to members of the family if they happen to be around. Then, after being shown into the lounge (*kyakuma*, or "guest room") each member of the family will be introduced to you formally. Don't be alarmed if elderly members of the family bow particularly low: you are the honored guest. As a foreigner, you will not be expected to reciprocate to the same extent.

"*Hajimemashite*" is the phrase used when meeting someone for the first time.

Typical words of welcome are: "*Yo koso irasshaimashita*" and "*Irasshaimase*" (as you will also hear in a restaurant).

You can reply quite simply by saying "*Hajimemashite*" back, and for extra politeness, add "*Dozo yoroshiku.*" (The whole phrase meaning: "I'm meeting you for the first time. I shall look forward to your kindness.")

---

those with children, do not typically go out together in the evenings to attend functions or dinners, or even just for relaxation. Thus, invitations may be accepted but often enough there is a "no-show" by the wife who will stay at home because she is embarrassed, pleading she has a cold. As we have seen, the Japanese prefer not to entertain at home

Visitors should never allow themselves to think that if they persist they can "break the mold" of centuries-old traditions and mind-sets: it only results in distress on both sides, and sometimes tears. This rule of thumb also applies in the case of the Western idea of "friendship." It is, of course, impossible to impose a Western-style relationship within a Japanese context and assume the same outcomes—especially in matters of the heart.

Finally, if you go to visit someone at home, it is good to take a small gift, ensuring that it is nicely wrapped of course (regardless of the occasion, the quality of wrapping is *always* important!)— cakes, biscuits, flowers, and fruit are ideal. And remember, the Japanese often do not unwrap gifts as soon as they are received.

BUSINESS BRIEFING

THE JAPANESE ECONOMY

Following the bursting of the Japanese "bubble economy" at the end of the 1980s, Japan's business environment in the first two decades of the twenty-first century has been facing major challenges and continues to do so. In 2012, after some twenty years of deflation (and more recently four recessions in five years), Shinzo Abe was elected prime minister and immediately announced his recovery plan for Japan. It was to be known henceforth as "Abenomics", summarised by his so-called "Three Arrows" consisting of 1. Looser monetary policy from the Bank of Japan (BoJ); 2. A fiscal boost by increasing spending on public works; 3. Fundamental structural reform to stimulate the economy and make it more productive.

It soon became apparent that without all three arrows finding their target more or less at the same time Abenomics would certainly fail. Failure, in fact, is almost assured because of fundamental issues that are unlikely to be resolved in the short or even medium term. Among the biggest issues is the huge problem of labor shortage because of the shrinking workforce, which means lack of construction workers. (According to the ManpowerGroup, 2015 survey, 83 percent of employers in Japan are struggling to hire new people—this is more than double the global average.) Adding to "recovery" frustrations is the downturn in China and the global economic slowdown generally, as well as a less than encouraging domestic outlook. "Spend some of your record cash piles on increased wages and investment," urges Prime Minister Abe; but such pleas continue to be ignored by business because of lack of confidence in both Abenomics and the fragility of both domestic and international trade.

Japan also continues to face the huge task of transforming an archaic and intransigent civil service that is inhibiting fundamental reforms to the way Japan governs itself.

Yet, despite the gloom, as noted in the Introduction, albeit gradually, potentially significant changes are slowly taking place that could have a positive outcome in the medium and longer term, particularly within the functioning of the *keiretsu*—the huge conglomerates, including the major banks, that dominate the Japanese economy. These include various forms of collaboration and share disposal that would have been unheard of in the past. For example, out of the original eight car manufacturers in Japan, only three today remain wholly owned. Even more significantly, foreign direct investment in Japan (FDI) rose from $3.2 billion in 1997 to $24.5 billion in 2008. But by 2013 its FDI ratio to GDP had slowed considerably to 3.5 percent— the lowest in developed countries where the average was 34 percent.

However, in acknowledging Japan's current socio-economic difficulties, it is easy to be persuaded, as some commentators are, that the country is in terminal decline. This, of course, makes no sense in the broader context of Japan's ongoing economic, industrial, and technological development: Japan is still a technological giant whose companies are at the forefront of innovation and application, including space; Japan's popular culture and entertainment industries expressed, for example, in *anime*, fashion, films, *manga*, pop music, and video games are hugely popular internationally. Japanese "high end" manufactures, from cars to camcorders, are still the products of choice around the world. However, as demand falls for traditional consumer electronics like TVs and personal computers, Sharp, the electronics, giant, for example, that makes screens for Apple i-phones is soon to launch display screens that can be shaped into various forms, including circular TVs, and remains one of the world's leading manufacturers for displays in cars and aircraft. Panasonic, meanwhile, is supplying the batteries for US electric car-maker Tesler

In 2014 the Nobel Prize in Physics went to three Japanese scientists for their work in developing blue light-emitting diodes, a symbolic achievement in the wider context of Japan's vigorous R&D environment, even though government is currently favoring so-called "strategic" research that offers more immediate benefits to industry and society, but possibly at the expense of basic research.

Furthermore, despite its language difficulties, more than ever Japan now engages actively in international affairs and contributes significantly to third-world aid programs. It has also emerged as an important contributor to Overseas Development Aid for environmental protection to China and other developing countries, and has become a leading player in key global environmental policy matters, not least climate change.

SOME INTRODUCTORY "ESSENTIALS"

Because of the importance to the Japanese of relationships—it is always "who you know," and within what circle, not "what you know"—an introduction by a go-between who knows both parties to a new business contact is a fundamental requirement and ensures the best starting point.

Punctuality is seen as an expression of good manners; thus, to arrive at a meeting late is to lose face and even to cause a degree of resentment, as well as undermine your perceived status. Furthermore, there is nothing to be gained in offering excuses, especially about traffic conditions, because everybody has to deal with that. (Even if you are a first-time visitor, you will be expected to know these things.) Profuse apologies and a humble demeanor are more appropriate.

Dress is also important. Japan has not yet adopted the tie-free, casual environment increasingly common in the USA and UK, and is unlikely to do so; smartness continues to matter. Flashy colors are also best avoided, given that the typical Japanese suit is dark blue with white shirt and bland tie. The Japanese word for suit is *sebiro*, which comes from "Savile Row"—the heartland of London's "gentleman" tailors. Allied with all of this is good deportment. If your bearing is too relaxed or laid back, it might be interpreted as lack of respect or even "crooked spirit."

Having said that, there was a brief flirtation with business fashion under prime minister Junichiro Koizumi (2001–6), well known for his

EXCHANGING BUSINESS CARDS (MEISHI)

- After shaking hands (most probably) or bowing (or occasionally both), hand over your business card with a slight bow, receiving one in return from your new acquaintance. (Visitors generally hand over their business card first.) Make sure that you present your card the right way up so that it can be read immediately.
- Your new acquaintance may hiss throug his teeth while studying your card. This show that you are an important person. Remember, your *meishi* is your "face" and thus an extremely personal item.
- Take your time to study the card received, and if it is in Japanese only, don't be embarrassed to ask for a translation of it.
- The Japanese always show the family name first, followed by the given or personal name. It is rare for Japanese to use given names among strangers, so get used to identifying the family name first and then add the word -*san;* thus Morita-san. (You will be referred to as Smith-san, *san* being the closest equivalent to Mr., Mrs., or Ms.)
- Once seated, it is good manners to keep the card in view on the table, or on the armrest of your chair.
- Finally, take the trouble to pocket it (in your wallet or *meishi* card holder) with some indication that it is of value to you.
- At the end of the day, add key words to the cards you have received so that you can readily identify who was who (including particulars of job function) at a future date, but don't ever write on the card in front of the person, and don't put *meishi* in your shirt or rear-trouser pocket.

> - Special *meishi* albums are available at stationery stores; these will prove an invaluable source of reference in the future.
>
> **REMEMBER:** In Japan, the business card is a key link in the "connections chain"; don't lose it, and make sure that you understand the status of the person who gave it to you (ask others if necessary). There will be many occasions when you will need to show your cards to others.

flamboyant suits and ties, who late in his premiership introduced what was called "Cool Biz." Following the government's decision to reduce carbon emissions from air conditioners during the summer months by setting them at 82.4 °F (28 °C)), he recommended a "no tie and jacket" campaign to compensate for higher office temperatures. The "Cool Biz" campaign never really took off (actually causing much confusion) and with few exceptions it soon became "business [dress] as usual." How much office workers' efficiency, however, suffers as a result of the higher temperatures has not been measured.

Also relevant in this context is the use of fragrances and deodorants. Body odor and cleanliness as we have seen is a sensitive issue. The Japanese generally do not use much in the way of perfumes, colognes, and aftershaves, except discreetly. High-powered fragrances, therefore, that leave "a trail" are best avoided, certainly during the business day. Equally, body piercing and tattoos are best kept discreetly hidden.

The Japanese value group solidarity enormously, so be ready to be met on arrival and seen off on departure.* You may well witness "sending off" gatherings at railway stations and airports, which can be extremely moving events. In the case of the departure of a senior manager to a new post elsewhere, the gathering may well conclude with a roar of "*banzai!*" ("hip, hip, hooray!") three times as a mark of affection and good luck.

When introduced, Japanese businessmen will first exchange business cards (*meishi*). Make sure you have your own right from the start of your visit, ideally with a translation in Japanese on the reverse. Check with your airline about this service well before departure; if the timing just isn't right, then arrange for the cards to be printed by your hotel as soon as you have checked in. Remember, without a business card in Japan you don't exist!

ASPECTS OF COMMUNICATION

English is the accepted lingua franca in Japan, although, of course, there are skilled speakers in other European and world languages, depending on a particular company's business activities and dealings. Many of the people you are likely to meet in a Japanese business context will have been specially chosen to interact with foreigners and for their knowledge of English. There will be others at the meeting, in more senior positions, who may only communicate to their interlocutor in Japanese, but who may well understand English far better than they can speak it.

Do not be surprised if you are outnumbered. In large companies, you will see a correlation between

---

* Because of the considerable time involved in getting to and from Narita Airport, you could always suggest a rendezvous at the Tokyo Station Narita Express platform.

age and seniority. This is because of the employment system and Japanese ideas about the importance of age. Some foreign companies make the mistake of sending young managers to important meetings. This is not appreciated.

Be prepared for lengthy translations of your comments, and for the side-conferences among the Japanese present that may follow. It is important not to be intimidated by this procedure, but to remain relaxed and focused. Although you may not speak the language, you can demonstrate by your body language that you are still an active participant.

Speak slowly and as clearly as possible, but not too slowly and without raising your voice, which might cause offense. But beware always that many misunderstandings are possible, even in an apparently free-flowing exchange—some arising because of nuances of language, different perceptions, and variables in body language.

When ushered into a room, sit at the place indicated by your host (you will invariably be directed where to sit), since the seat of honor and other positions in decreasing order of importance are usually predetermined; this is particularly the case in the traditional Japanese house.

The Japanese generally prefer discussing business in the hotel's reception area and not in your room. If it is not feasible to do so, suggest moving to a coffee shop or bar. The Japanese seem to accept that they may be overhead by strangers in such places—much in the same way that they "hear" but don't "listen" or "look" but don't "see."

Visitors will quickly become aware of the importance of routine communication in Japan, both on a micro and macro level. Within departments there are constant meetings, and with those out of the office constant communications. And for those separated from their reference group—on domestic, or especially, international assignments—the Japanese tend to telephone or write back to base frequently, even if there is little news. This "umbilical link" is seen as fundamental to the maintenance of positive, ongoing smooth relations. On a macro level, there is sometimes a feeling that Japan is communicating with itself twenty-four hours a day; it is no surprise, therefore, that Japan rapidly became one of the world's top cell-phone users in the late 1990s.

There is no harm, therefore, in copying this custom with your Japanese group, especially after you return home. Photos, cards at Christmas and/or New Year, are reminders that you still care.

WOMEN IN BUSINESS

Although there have been some high-profile appointments (and disappointments) of women in business and government, generally speaking women continue to be discriminated against in the Japanese workplace and continue to earn earn 30–40 percent less than their male colleaugues. Indeed, the male-orientated imperative within Japanese society is such that it is difficult to see this situation changing, except very gradually over time. Although Prime Minister Abe's "Abenomics" plan includes encouraging more women back to work after bringing up their family, few believe this will have much impact on the 70 percent who don't.

INSIGHTS INTO "THE BOW"

It has been said that the Japanese bow represents the most readily identifiable form of *conscious* nonverbal communication. Bowing communicates respect by avoiding eye contact (unlike Westerners who seek it). In bowing, you are communicating at a profound level.

Bowing communicates a range of different nonverbal messages, such as initial greetings, farewells, gratitude, acknowledgment, apology, degree of familiarity, comparative social or corporate rank, and gender. These messages are refined by the depth of the bow, the position of the hands (held in front or by the side), the frequency of the bow, and who initiates it.

Potentially, there are 7–8 million "workers" that could be added to Japan's depleted workforce relatively quickly.

Western businesswomen therefore can expect to find few, if any, counterparts in Japan, and may themselves be viewed as an oddity in the overwhelmingly male-dominated surroundings of business and after-hours entertainment.

As with her Western male colleagues, a Western businesswoman during her initial stay is likely to be treated as a high-status *gaijin okyakyu-sama* (honorable foreign guest) first and foremost; subsequently, she may well find herself being discriminated against because of her sex, and not always that subtly; the final indignity can sometimes result in more hostile behavior by Japanese male colleagues.

It is unlikely, however, even in the role of honorable guest, that she would be invited to after-hours drinking sessions, and especially not to the more intimate parties involving female entertainers that important visitors and clients might be treated to after the evening's formal party draws to a close.

Nevertheless, it is a reassuring fact that the molestation of women who venture out alone in Japan is a rare event. By contrast, during parties, Japanese males, later pleading drunkenness (see page 79), may sometimes become over-amorous, or start fondling or pinching Western women. If the woman concerned objects promptly, this should ideally lead to apologies and no further contact.

Since the first edition of this book in 2003, and despite record numbers entering the workforce, very little has changed for women in business, including representation in the boardroom. Molestation of women alone continues to be rare, whereas Japan Railways has introduced some women-only carriages on the underground during the rush-hours to help limit the extent of molestation by men on trains (*chikan*), which remains a big problem.

Since Japanese wives are generally excluded when their husbands entertain on business, Western wives are rarely invited either (see pages 136–7). However, the "internationalization" of Japan's business environment is gradually bringing about carefully managed formal occasions to which foreign wives are invited. Nevertheless, if they do go, they should not expect to be engaged in scintillating conversation by their usually tongue-tied male Japanese hosts. Nor are they likely (except at, say, Embassy functions) to meet the hosts' wives.

Dress for women, as for the men, is typically conservative, consisting of dark suits or dresses (tights are always worn). Given the lower average height of Japanese women, avoid high heels and go for "sensible" shoes. Formality is expected at all times and thus overfamiliarity, terms of endearment, and diminutives should be avoided always. Modest make-up and discreet perfume are also recommended.

UNDERSTANDING "NO"

To encourage harmony, Japanese conversation mostly allows the participants to agree. Consequently, contentious issues are avoided. Refusals, if necessary, tend to be indirect, and here is where it can be especially difficult for new arrivals—reading the convoluted hesitations, drawing of breath, head movements, and phrases such as "frankly speaking" (widely used) and "it may be difficult." The word "no" in Japanese (*ii-e*) sounds harsh and is rarely used. Instead, get used to (and use) "well, maybe" (*kamo shiremasen*), or apply the art of pausing. The pause is often equivalent to "no"—just as a non-reply mostly means "no." Non-reply to correspondence, faxes, and e-mails is one of the most difficult aspects of Japanese behavior for Westerners to accommodate: it becomes especially difficult to accept when it involves someone you believe you know well or reasonably well. Persisting beyond a certain point is futile and it is best to move on. Equally, don't automatically take "yes" for an answer in the Western sense.

Also, be aware that increasing numbers of Japanese are conversant with Western character traits and expectations—in particular the "direct approach"—and may lead you to believe that business will be done on that basis. However, this is unlikely to be the case, and you should always remind yourself that, pleasing though it is to be on a positive "one-to-one" with a Japanese colleague or business partner, the fact remains that this is likely to be purely an intellectual accommodation of Western behavior. Conversely, however linguistically accomplished you may be, and however well you may "know" Japan, you will always be perceived as an outsider for the simple reason that you are not Japanese.

THE SOUND OF SILENCE

The Japanese love silence and actually "communicate" with it. Westerners tend to be afraid of silence and instinctively seek to fill it. Thus, "silence pauses" at meetings, or even in informal conversations, should be respected for what they are meant to be—pauses for thought and reflection, or an opportunity to move to a new topic in a gracious way.

Above all, "silent pauses" should never be broken with a joke or funny story!

It is also worth remembering that sometimes communication with a Japanese you have known breaks down and "silence" ensues—for no apparent reason. It may be that the person concerned does not know how to respond to your last communication, or it may be that, deep down, it is just too much effort. Further reminders or follow-ups are usually just a waste of time and it is better to move on.

UNDERSTANDING "YES"

Equally, it is vitally important to understand the meaning of the word "yes" (*hai*) in Japanese. For most of the time, *hai* is interjected as a supportive listening word and simply means "Yes, I hear you." Sometimes, for emphatic acknowledgment, *hai, hai* is used. It would be highly unlikely, however, for *hai* to be used in response to the question: "So, we are agreed on the deal, then?" unless it iwas followed up with an enunciation of what the deal consisted of.

CONSENSUS

As we have seen, the Japanese greatly prize harmony (*wa*) and instinctively seek consensus, with the team achieving things, rather than any one individual within it. Thus, consensus discussion (*nemawashi*) and seeking agreement (*ringi-sho*) are routine processes at all levels of society, but above all, of course, in business and politics. Reaching corporate agreement, therefore, on any proposal almost certainly takes far longer than the Western world is used to, because other colleagues and departments must be consultedalso. This may, of course, be different in smaller, owner-controlled companies.

However, it has often been noted that although reaching a decision in Japan may take a long time, the implementation can be surprisingly quick. Typically, therefore, a number of levels of Japanese management and skill competencies will be present at a meeting, or on a fact-finding initial visit, precisely because all the levels involved in the implementation of any decision to proceed will have to be involved in the agreement (*ringi-sho*) process.

There are obvious drawbacks in this approach for Japan, especially in the international arena (even with backroom "back-up"!) when votes are required on the day regarding a particular motion—whether it be after a debate in the United Nations or at an academic conference.

HOW TO ENGAGE WITH THE JAPANESE: INSIGHTS FROM A TRADE MISSION

In some cases, members of a mission found that they could succeed more quickly when they understood what was required on the Japanese side.

- Recognize the importance of strong personal relationships and do not rely soley on written contracts to do business.
- Complaints from Japanese customers should be used as a learning opportunity and be responded to in the positive spirit intended.
- Rather than see complaints as a negative, see silence as a negative, insofar as silence means the Japanese side has given up on trying to bring about improvement.
- Understand the importance of "after 5:00 p.m." business discussions—the reason why Asahi and Kirin beers play such an important part of Japanese business life.

[With thanks to Ivor Cohen]

A "Communications" Story

The new marketing executive for East Asia wanted feedback from her Japanese agent, so she rang him. "Ho, Koji; how are things going?" she greeted him. Koji replied haltingly that things were fine. She asked him what he thought of the new product line. Koji didn't reply. There was a long pause. Embarrassed by the silence, she asked him again what his opinion was. Koji reluctantly asked a question about product specifications. The marketing executive pressed him. "I'd really like to know what you think." Apologetically and reluctantly, Koji mentioned a criticism of the product that he had heard. The marketing executive ended the conversation with the dissatisfied feeling that she had handled it all wrongly.

On the whole, as we have seen, the Japanese prefer to volunteer collective opinions after discussion, not individual opinions, and certainly not to strangers on the phone. Feedback is considered, collectively reviewed, and is, above all, consensual.

By definition, therefore, feedback is rarely instant and individual. The Japanese agent probably felt a keen loss of face—both for himself by his embarrassment, and for her for putting him in that situation.

Had the marketing executive been more experienced she might have:

(1) been a little more respectful and deliberate, while remaining friendly.

(2) not demanded instant opinions but signaled the importance of getting some feedback on the product's reception in Japan.

(3) suggested that when Koji-san had had the opportunity to examine the product in greater detail she would value his team's opinion.

She would have had an answer within a very few days!

OTHER DOS AND DON'TS

- Always use "we" not "I." You will often hear the phrase *ware ware nihonjin* ("we Japanese"). Japan is not an "I" culture, and it is best to recognize that from the outset.

- Always avoid situations where there could be loss of face and consequent embarrassment.

- Don't reject anything out of hand. Give yourself time to think about the proposal and use phrases such as "I'll study that," or "I'll look forward to discussing it further."

- Don't confront people or attempt to force decisions they cannot make; and don't get angry (it shows a profound lack of self-respect and you lose face).

- Always choose the indirect approach whenever possible because the Japanese are most comfortable with this.

- The Japanese are an intensely visual people; so have diagrams to hand out whenever you think it could be helpful.

- Restrained body language will always be preferred to excited gesticulation, touching (don't touch!—except "after hours"), and noisy outbursts.

- Don't try to make routine eye contact; like so much else in Japan the direct approach is avoided.

- Don't expect to return to the office the morning after a good night out and relive the great time you all had. This is simply not done—and for the compartmentally driven Japanese mind, anything that happens "after six" doesn't exist! In any event, for the Japanese, such fun times are often best forgotten!

- Don't assume that because you are a foreigner "company regulations" only apply to the Japanese staff; although allowances will be made, your "esteemed bank account" will be greatly augmented in proportion to the efforts at integration you are seen to be making. This also applies to learning the language (see Chapter 10).

- In your relations with expatriate Japanese, don't assume that the quality of your perceived friendship will carry through once the person concerned returns to Japan. In the ordinary course of things, the Japanese person has to reorientate him/herself as well as reintegrate into Japanese society, which can sometimes be very difficult. Of course, you may want to make every effort possible to keep the friendship going through correspondence, e-mail, and so on. But if it doesn't work out, you will know why.

chapter ten

LANGUAGE & COMMUNICATION

The popular Japanese expression "*Ganbatte kudasai*" ("Please do your best!" or "Go for it!") is particularly appropriate in a discussion on the Japanese language. It may be one of the hardest languages to master, certainly in its written form, but Japanese is now recognized as one of the world's important *modern* languages. Self-evidently, learning even a little spoken Japanese will make visiting or living in Japan much easier. In addition, the Japanese respond warmly to anyone attempting to learn their language—indeed, the effort to hold the simplest day-to-day conversations yields disproportionate rewards in terms of Japanese affirmation and practical outcomes.

Of course, it is entirely possible to live in metropolitan Japan without speaking a word of Japanese, but it would be expecting a lot of your hosts and Japanese colleagues to get everything right in English all of the time.

In addition to the more than 127 million people living in Japan, it is worth noting that Japanese is also spoken abroad wherever Japanese people have settled—in North and South America (the biggest Japanese population outside Japan is in Brazil) and in Hawaii—and by an estimated three million people around the world, including many Chinese, as well as schoolchildren in North America, the UK, Australia, and New Zealand, for whom Japanese sometimes forms part of the curriculum.

Adult literacy and numeracy in Japan is virtually 100 percent, the highest in the world. How has this come about? Much is said about the rigor of the Japanese education system, where rote learning is still a fundamental teaching tool and the "Three Rs" (reading, writing, and arithmetic) continue to dominate the curriculum. But the learning of the language itself is surely a major factor in terms of advancing both the intellect and the memory.

STRUCTURE OF THE LANGUAGE

The Japanese script uses a mixture of Chinese characters or ideograms (*kanji*) plus two phonetic "shorthand" systems (known as syllabaries)—*katakana* and *hiragana*, which are derived from *kanji* and contain forty-six symbols each. *Katakana* is used to write foreign names and loan words, and *hiragana* is used on railway signboards, sometimes on menus, and so on. Roman script (*romaji*) is also used.

The number of *kanji* in regular use is approximately 2,000. These must be mastered by the end of lower secondary school—compulsory education finishes at the age of fifteen, but practically every child in Japan (95 percent) goes on to upper secondary/senior high school for a further three years. The two syllabaries also have to be mastered at school, of course. Furthermore, the Arabic numerals have to be learned, as well as writing with brush and ink, which involves a considerable investment in time, particularly at primary school.

READING THE RAILWAY SIGNS

A typical railway signboard will give the name of the station in a mixture of scripts for the convenience of everyone (including youngsters who haven't yet mastered enough *kanji*, and foreigners who can't read Japanese). Usually, the top row of characters will be in *kanji*, and below that will be *hiragana* and then *romaji* (Roman script). At the very bottom are left and right arrows with *kanji* above pointing to the previous station (with name) and the next station (with name).

Japanese does not fit easily into any of the "family trees" of the world's languages. On the one hand, it has a grammatical affinity with Korean and Central Asian languages; on the other, when spelled out, it looks strikingly similar to some Polynesian languages. In fact, one of the most provocative theories about the origins of Japanese is that it is a Central Asian language spoken with a Polynesian accent—in the same way that French is a form of Latin spoken with a Gallic accent.

Unlike Chinese (from which many Japanese *kanji* were originally imported) with its formidable array of tonal levels, Japanese is not an inflected language and consequently is comparatively easy to pronounce (see over), which is encouraging for beginners. However, every word of Japanese you learn will be a "one off" item of vocabulary. There are no familiar linguistic landmarks and word families as there are in European languages! But there are rewards for your efforts. For example, unlike European scripts, Japanese is written vertically (top to bottom, right to left), making it very easy to read the title of a book on a bookshop shelf without having to turn your head ninety degrees! Of course, a Japanese book, by definition, is also "back to front!"

Clearly, therefore, there is no shortcut to learning Japanese. Mastery of the language will require *daily* study and revision over several years. But for those looking to achieve "survival" Japanese (in both speaking and comprehension), determined application over six months is usually the agreed time frame.

Fortunately for beginners, a "helping hand" is available: the Japanese are also extremely fond of using loan words from Western languages, with English words predominating (see opposite).

PRONUNCIATION

Although the pronunciation of Japanese is relatively easy, there are some quicksands in comprehension if you fail to grasp the difference between the long vowel and the short vowel. In Romaji the long vowel is indicated by using a line (macron) above the *ō* and *ū* . For example, *shujin* with a short *u* means "my husband," whereas *shūjin* with a long *ū* means "jailbird." *Kyōto* is Kyoto, the ancient capital; whereas *kyotō* is "a big shot," and *kyōtō* is an "assistant principal" of a school or college.

Also, it is important to pronounce the vowels in a dipthong quite distinctly. Thus, the Japanese surname Maeda is pronounced *ma-e-da* (not rhyming with "Maida" as in Maida Vale in London); "*geisha*," on the other hand, is usually not split into *ge-i-sha*, but pronounced with a long *ē*, *gēsha*; whereas *maiko*, the apprentice *geisha*, is pronounced *ma-i-ko*.

Finally, the *e* at the end of a word in Japanese is sounded, thus *saké* (rice wine), *netsuké* (the famous miniature carved toggles), and Nakasoné (the former prime minister). Also, remember that, for the most part, Japanese nouns do not distinguish between singular and plural; so the word *hon* means both book and books, *denwa* is telephone and telephones.

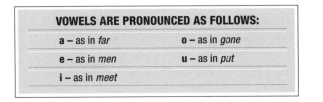

VOWELS ARE PRONOUNCED AS FOLLOWS:	
a – as in *far*	**o** – as in *gone*
e – as in *men*	**u** – as in *put*
i – as in *meet*	

The "L" and "R" Problem

Famously, Japanese airlines have had to cope
with the joke about staff wishing their customers
"a nice fright" on their journey to "Rondon"—
the point being that the Japanese language does
not distinguish between the "l" and "r" sounds,
and invariably the "r" option is selected for ease
of delivery. As teachers of English as a foreign
language know, the "l" sound for Japanese students
is not easy to achieve, and is basically a problem
involving the placement of the tongue in the mouth.

SOME "IMPORTED" WORDS

As we have seen, the Japanese have imported loan
words, mostly from English, in order to expand
their contemporary vocabulary and meet the needs
of modern society. Here is a selection that may
bring a ready smile to native speakers of English!
(Remember that the Japanese often have to add in
the vowels "*ro*" and "*ru*" to render the loan words
pronounceable in Japanese!)

arukoru alcohol; **asupirin** aspirin; **azukaru**
to look after, take care of (belongings); **ba** bar;
baggu bag; **butsu** boots; **chekku auto** check-out;
chiizu cheese; **chokoreto** chocolate; **dababru**

double (room); **departo** department store; **dorai kurliningu** dry cleaning; **eakon** air conditioning; **erebeta** elevator; **fasuto fudo** fast food; **furonto** reception desk (hotel); **gurasu** glass; **handobaggu** handbag; **hoteru** hotel; **hotto doggu** hot dog; **kohii shoppu** coffee shop; **kuroku** cloakroom; **meron** mellon; **nekkuresu** necklace; **pasupoto** passport; **purinto** print; **puroguramu** program; **rabu hoteru** love hotel; **rajio** radio; **raunji ba** lounge bar; **rentaka** rental car; **resutoran** restaurant; **sarariiman** businessman; **serusuman** sales person; **shinguru** single (room); **sofuto dorinku** soft drink; **tabako** cigarette; **terebi** television; **uisukii** whiskey; **wa puro** word processor; **yusu hosuteru** youth hostel.

CONCLUSION

No single phenomenon can encapsulate the essence of a country, least of all a sophisticated culture like that of Japan, but it is fun to explore the options. We have considered the singular nature of Japan as a country and people "apart," with a distinctive language and religion, and a way of life that is informed by a groupist or consensus-driven philosophy, underpinned by many and varied protocols governing personal relationships and social exchange.

We have glimpsed Japan's unique artistic heritage, and the remarkable way in which the past coexists with the present, and the natural world continues to inform modern life.

A wonderful example of this can be found in Japanese poetry, in a seventeen-syllable form of verse known as *haiku*. The great master of this particular form of poetry was Matsuo Basho, who died in 1694. *Haiku*, which is rooted in the natural world, is universally appreciated in Japan, and reinforced by numerous annual *haiku* events and competitions. This is one of Basho's most famous *haiku*:

> *Listen! A frog*
> *Jumping into the stillness*
> *Of an ancient pond!*
> (Transl., Dorothy Britton)

Appendix: Some Useful Words and Phrases

The following are among those frequently required by the visitor:

Good morning **ohayo gozaimas'**
Good day **konichi wa**
Good evening **konban wa**
Good night (on retiring) **o-yasumi nasai**
Good-bye **sayonara**
Meeting someone for the first time **hajimemashite**
Welcome! **Irasshaimase!**
Thank you **domo arigato** (or simply **domo** or **arigato'**)
Thank you very much – **domo arigato gozaimashita**
Hot, isn't it? **atsui des' ne!**
Cold, isn't it? **samui des' ne!**
Yes, I'm listening **hai, hai**
Yes, I agree **hai, so des'**
Please (help yourself) **dozo**
Please give me ... **o kudasai ...**
On starting a meal **itadakimas'**
Cheers! **kampai!**
Excuse me **sumimasen**
My name is [Paul] – [Paul] **des'** (after name)
Pleased to meet you **dozo yoroshiku**
You're welcome **do itashimash'te**
I don't understand **wakarimasen**
I don't understand Japanese **Nihongo ga wakarimasen**
Please call a taxi **takushii o yonde kudasai**
To the right **migi**
To the left **hidari**
Straight ahead **massugu**
Stop **tomatte**

Here **koko**
There **asoko**
To attract attention (e.g. in a restaurant) **Sumimasen!**
When meal arrives, say **go-chiso sama** *(what a feast!)*
It's beautiful (scenery), isn't it! **kirei desu ne!**
Hello (on the phone) **Moshi, moshi**
Telephone call **o-denwa**

Meals

Breakfast **asa-gohan**
Lunch **hiru-gohan**
Dinner **ban-gohan**

Numbers

one *i-chi*
two *ni*
three *san*
four *shi (yon)*
five *go*
six *roku*
seven *shi-chi, na-na*
eight *ha-chi*
nine *ku, kyu*
ten *ju*

Office

President/chairman **shacho**
Department head **bucho**
Section head **kacho**
Subsection head **kakaricho**

Further Reading

The BusinessTravellers' Handbook to Japan.
London: Stacey International, 2009.

Clarke, P. B. *A Bibliography of Japanese New Religious Movements.* Japan Library. London: 1999.

Harper, P. *The Insider's Guide to Saké.* Tokyo: Kodansha International, 1998.

Hendry, J. *Understanding Japanese Society.* London: Croom Helm, 1987.

Jansen, Marius B. *The Making of Modern Japan.* Cambridge, MA: Harvard University Press, 2002.

Kimura, Harumi (ed.). *Living Japan: Essays on Everyday Life in Contemporary Society.* Folkestone, Kent: Global Oriental, 2009.

Lonely Planet Japan. London: Lonely Planet, 2015

Pocket World in Figures. London: The Economist, 2015.

Plutschow, H. *Matsuri: Festivals of Japan.* Folkestone, Kent: Japan Library, 1996.

Reader, I., et al. *Japanese Religions Past & Present.* Folkestone, Kent: Japan Library, 1993.

Reischauer, E. *The Story of a Nation.* Tokyo and Vermont: Charles E. Tuttle, 1970.

Richie, Donald. *Lafcadio Hearn's Japan: An Anthology of His Writings on the Country and its People.* North Clarendon, VT: Tuttle Classics, 2007.

Richmond, Simon. *The Rough Guide to Japan.* London: Penguin Books, 2014.

Rogers, Hiromi T. *Anjin – The Life and Times of Samurai William Adams, 1564–1620. As Seen Through Japanese Eyes.* Folkestone, Kent: Renaissance Books, 2016.

Storry, R. *A History of Modern Japan.* London: Penguin Books, 1982.

Language Guides

http://www.japanvisitor.com/japanese-culture/language/lang-basic-japanese

Clarke, H. D. B., and Motoko Hanamura. *Colloquial Japanese. The Complete Course for Beginners.* London: Routledge, 2003.

In-Flight Japanese. New York: Living Language, 2001.

Japanese. A Complete Course. New York: Living Language, 2005.

Japanese Business Companion. The Language Guide for Business. New York: Living Language, 2003.

culture smart! japan

Index